GLENN MILLER DISCOGRAPHY

A

GLENN MILLER DISCOGRAPHY

AND

BIOGRAPHY

Compiled and Written by

STEPHEN F. BEDWELL

Edited and with additional material by

Geoffrey E. Butcher

REVISED EDITION

LONDON:
GLENN MILLER APPRECIATION SOCIETY
3, GT. PERCY STREET, W.C.1
1956

First published, December 1955
Reprinted with additions, January 1956

Printed by H. E. Warne, Ltd., St. Austell
Cornwall, England

DISCOGRAPHER'S INTRODUCTION

The purpose of this booklet is to provide a basic reference handbook for the Glenn Miller collector. Prepared during my ten years of active collecting, I feel that it surpasses any existing works on Glenn Miller. It is, however, still incomplete, and probably inaccurate in many places. Space will not allow all of the information gathered to be published. Therefore, a selection of the information which I felt would be of the most value has been made.

The booklet has been divided into five sections.

The first is a short biography.

The second is a discography, with comments and various related information of Glenn Miller, trombonist, from 1925 to 1937.

The third section is a discography of the famous Glenn Miller civilian orchestras of 1935 to 1942. I have included in this section notes on one night stands, radio programmes, and soloists. Included too, are all known reissues of Miller discs throughout the world. I have no doubt that many of Glenn's recordings were issued in other countries, and on other labels than those mentioned. Where the exact timing of "air checks" is known this is given so that collectors may date, or catalogue their "air checks."

Section four deals with the great Glenn Miller Army Air Force Orchestra both at home and abroad.

The final section is devoted to the "LP" and "EP" reissues of recordings, the issues of "air checks," and the new "Glenn Miller Moonlight Serenade" transcriptions.

I had hoped to have my collection of photographs of the Glenn Miller orchestra published with the discography, but the costs were prohibitive.

In closing I should like to offer my sincere thanks to the hundreds of collectors who have added contributions to the work, although I am sorry to say that there are one or two who have, for one reason or another, failed to produce information which they had available.

Special thanks are due to Mr. Donald W. Haynes who very kindly sent a listing of the new Glenn Miller transcriptions, and corrected the manuscript, and Mr. Geoffrey E. Butcher who added new data prior to publication.

STEPHEN F. BEDWELL

June 1954.
49 Highcroft Road,
Toronto 8, Ontario,
Canada.

EDITOR'S NOTE.

It has always been the aim of the Miller Society to publish a complete Glenn Miller Discography, and work on one was far advanced when Dr. Bedwell offered us his own admirable compilation. It proved to be more detailed than our own, so we decided to publish it in preference to ours.

Dr. Bedwell was unfortunately compelled to give up work on his Discography in July 1954, having completed the book as at that date ready for publication. My part in the enterprise has been limited to revising the manuscript in respect of the multitude of commercial record issues since that time (American and British, plus those of a few other countries), adding about one third of Section IV, revising the civilian Miller Band personnels, and seeing the book through the press. So to Dr. Bedwell should be attributed all the credit and ninety per cent of the work for the book.

A word of explanation is due regarding the civilian Miller Band personnels for the period 1938 to 1942. For many years, almost the only details available were those published in the "New Hot Discography" (New York, Criterion Music Corporation, *and* Commodore Record Shop, 1948) and in various musical publications when the records were reviewed at the time of their original issue in the late 30's and early 40's. However, in course of time it became apparent that the information in the "New Hot Discography" was incomplete and, in some cases, inaccurate. Then, in the last two or three years, in the course of its research activities the G.M.A.S. obtained much new information from R.C.A. Victor and other sources, although some of the Victor information was conflicting in itself, some contradicted other known details, and some had frankly to be viewed with suspicion. Eventually, we obtained what amounted to five or six different accounts of the Miller Band personnels covering the four and a half years of the Band's existence, each account differing in varying degrees with regard to individual musicians and their dates of playing in the Band! Naturally, this has caused a great deal of correspondence between myself and R.C.A. Victor, and I can only express my thanks here for their helpfulness and indulgence in my efforts to arrive at the true sequence of the often-changing personnel of a Band of a bygone era. The task was made more difficult by the fact that the records concerned consist of the usual studio recordings and many radio broadcast extracts as well; further, it sometimes happened that some musicians played at recording sessions and not broadcasts, while others played on the air and not in the recording studios!

My task, therefore, was to correlate all this fresh personnel information with that assembled by Dr. Bedwell. This I have done with his agreement, and after much careful consideration of all the available evidence, diligent checking and cross-checking, and reference to periodicals of the time when the Miller Band was working, I have worked out what I believe to be as nearly a completely correct record of the personnel changes as is perhaps ever likely to be obtained now. As Victor have pointed out, ". . . . . getting an accurate list of the musicians who played at various restaurants and dance halls back in the 1930's is a tremendous undertaking." Where uncertainty still exists I have inserted Notes.

Thus, this Discography is an entirely new work, compiled from original sources and owing little or nothing to previous publications in the field. It still has a few gaps and possibly time will show small inaccuracies, so I shall be glad to receive corrections and additions that readers may care to submit.

One other point—in order that none of my sins shall be laid at Dr. Bedwell's door I have initialled all the Notes throughout the work for which I am responsible.

My warmest thanks are due to all those who have kindly submitted data for inclusion; to Mr. Paul Doye, my colleague in the G.M.A.S., for assistance; and, to my wife who has helped with much onerous checking, but who, most of all, has tolerated the whole thing for so long.

GEOFFREY E. BUTCHER
(*Editor, The Moonlight Serenader, Journal of the G.M.A.S.*)

October, 1955,
London, England.

RECORD LABEL ABBREVIATIONS

Symbol	*Name*	*Symbol*	*Name*
AFRS	Armed Forces Radio Service (16-in. Transcription)	MW	Montgomery Ward
		Od	Odeon
Ar	Ariel	OK	Okeh
Ba	Banner	Or	Oriole
BB	Bluebird (Canadian and US issues have same no.)	OWI	Office of War Information (12-in discs like V-Discs)
Bi	Biltmore	Pa	Parlophone
Br	Brunswick (Canadian discs when issued had US nos)	Pana	Panachord
		Pe	Perfect
CI	Collectors Item	Ph	Philips
Co	Columbia	Po	Polk
Cq	Conqueror	Poly	Polygon
De	Decca (Canadian and US issues have same no.)	Polyd	Polydor
		Rex	Rex
Epic	Epic	Ro	Romeo
GMMS	Glenn Miller's Moonlight Serenade (Transcriptions)	RZ	Regal Zonophone
		V-D	V-Disc (12-in—78 rpm discs produced for US Troops)
Gr	Gramophone (European HMV)		
Ha	Harmony	VdP	Voce del Padrone (Italian HMV)
HJCA	Hot Jazz Club of America		
HMV	His Master's Voice	Vi	Victor (Canadian and US issues have same nos.)
HRS	Hot Record Society		
May	Mayfair	Vo	Vocalion
Me	Meltone		

COUNTRY SUFFIXES

Suffix	*Country*	*Suffix*	*Country*
Au	Australia	G	Germany
C	Canada (Where issue no. differs from US no.)	I	India
		J	Japan
E	England	Sp	Spain
F	France	Sw	Switzerland

INSTRUMENT ABBREVIATIONS

Symbol	*Instrument*	*Symbol*	*Instrument*
AS	Alto Saxophone	S	Saxophone
BS	Baritone Saxophone	St	String Section
Bj	Banjo	TB	Trombone
B	Bass (String)	TP	Trumpet
Cello	Violon Cello	TS	Tenor Saxophone
Cls	Celeste	Tu	Tuba
Clt	Clarinet	Vla	Viola
C	Cornet	Vln	Violin
D	Drums	W	Woodwinds
F	Flute		
G	Guitar	a	Arranged By
P	Piano	Int	Introduced By
Rh	Rhythm Section	VR	Vocal Refrain

Notes.

1. The first issue number listed for any selection is the first issue.
2. Any reissues are listed in alphabetical order by label.
3. Playing times of broadcast performances ("airchecks") indicated thus (3: 01).

CONTENTS

SECTION I

A GLENN MILLER BIOGRAPHY

The Glenn Miller Story is truly a "rags-to-riches" narrative.

In Clarinda, Iowa, where his father, Lewis Elmer Miller, worked as a carpenter, Alton Glenn Miller was born on March 1, 1904. Five years later Glenn and his family moved to the Nebraska Dust Bowl to live in a primitive sod hut. Life was hard. Glenn and his family had to become pioneers, battling nature to survive. The summers were spent in constant dread of prairie fires which would destroy their home; the winters were lonely with Lewis Miller working in a town forty miles away. In these forsaken formative years Glenn spent most of his lonely hours dreaming, and developing the insatiable drive which stamped him as a man destined to succeed.

Lewis moved to North Platte, Nebraska, following five years of toil and poverty, to return to carpentry. More children were born here and Glenn, although still only a youngster, went to work.

"My first job was milking a cow for two dollars a week," he once recollected.

A later move to Grant City, Missouri, brought Glenn his first trombone. He was working as a butcher's errand boy when he noticed the old instrument propping up a cupboard in the cellar. Fascinated by the instrument, Glenn was presented with it by the butcher, who also offered to show him how to play it. Nearly "driving his father nuts practising trombone" Glenn soon mastered it and played in local concerts.

Glenn went to high school in Fort Morgan, Colorado, while supporting himself by doing odd jobs and working part-time in a sugar beet factory. Following graduation he joined his first band in Laramie, Wyoming. The band, whose leader is unknown, broke up after a year, and Glenn, desirous of obtaining more education, enrolled in the University of Colorado where he met his future wife, Helen Dorothy Burger. Glenn developed a craze for football while at university, and became an "all-state" left end. But his music was not forgotten, as he worked many one-night stands, among which was a short stay with Boyd Senter at the Albany Hotel in Denver.

On leaving college after a stay of two years Glenn travelled to the west coast to join Ben Pollack's Orchestra in November 1925. His first recordings were made with the Pollack band a year later for the Victor Gramophone Company, one medium of his later success. He is supposed to have cut some sides with the Original Wolverines about this time, but the evidence is inconclusive.

Leaving the Pollack organisation, Glenn joined Paul Ash's Paramount Theatre Orchestra in New York City. He stayed with Ash until October 7, 1928, when he married his College sweetheart, Helen Burger. Freelancing for the next five years Glenn cut many discs with such greats as Red Nichols and Benny Goodman. Much of this period was spent with pit bands in New York. During the two years following 1933 Glenn cut nearly one hundred sides with the Dorsey Brothers' Orchestra.

Miller was the organizing-arranging genius behind Ray Noble's first American orchestra, which is famous not only for the high quality of its music, but also for the unique fact that every member of that band became the leader of his own orchestra in the next few years. It was during this period that Glenn embarked on the only formal musical training of his career. Previously, durıng his early life at home, his mother, the former Mattie Lou Cavender, had taught him the language of music through the medium of hymnal melodies; but now he began his studies under the brilliant Dr. Joseph Schillinger, who had developed a mathematical approach to music. The inspiration for the "Miller Sound" was born under Dr. Schillinger's guidance.

The work with Noble crystallized Glenn's ideas about having his own band. Besides the success of the Noble crew, his arrangements were selling well, and he was more than just a competent musician. He found too, that he was not getting the results we wanted, and said:

"I was tired of arguing about arrangements, of having things come out differently from the way I wrote them. I wanted to hear my own ideas and the only way was to have my own crew.

Among his arrangements was an exercise written for Dr. Schillinger which employed a clarinet-tenor lead with balanced harmony filled in by the other saxes. Contrary to many stories the lead was written this way, and everyone liked it so much that Glenn finished the melody, and, calling it "Gone with the Wind" used it as his theme. When he recorded the tune in 1939 the title was changed to "Moonlight Serenade."

To be successful in the "Swing World" it was necessary to have a precision squad, which could out-manoeuver any other orchestra in any direction—be it sweet or swing. This was the type of orchestra which Glenn desired, and which he spent several years in building. In 1937 the New Haven Studios in New York listened to the first rehearsal of the Glenn Miller Orchestra, with Charlie Spivak, "Toots" Mondello and other expensive sidemen. The band opened under the auspices of the General Amusement Corporation at the Hotel New Yorker for a one-nighter. Other dates followed, but because of high expenses and arguments with the booking office and the sidemen, Miller fired all but four, and pla yed small dates while collecting another group of musicians—less expensive ones this time. Among these new musicians were some who were with the Orchestra until its breakup in 1942. Men like "Chummy" MacGregor, Tex Beneke, Paul Tanner, and Wilbur Schwartz rehearsed every bar in every arrangement a thousand times until it was impossible to make mistakes.

Because of this gruelling work Glenn got the name of a musical martinet and an over-zealous disciplinarian in the "Swing World," but there were several who saw the future of the new band and gave it many a helping hand. Foremost of these were Tommy Dorsey, Cy Shribman, and Mike Nidorf.

The nadir in the band's career came during a blizzard in New England when the cars stalled. They finally found a farm house and saved themselves from freezing. While trying to get warm Glenn wondered if it were worth while going on, but go on he did and was rewarded by success.

Within a few short weeks he had dates at the "Paradise" in New York, then the "Meadowbrook", perhaps the most famous roadhouse in the East, and, after a short road trip, the "Glen Island Casino" in New Rochelle, which is known as the "Cradle of Name Bands." Following his debut in a Carnegie Hall Concert in October, Miller began his now famous three-night-a-week Chesterfield shows on December 27, 1939. The band was now, literally, "The Sensation of the Nation."

Success on records followed, and perhaps the most successful, other than his theme, was "Chattanooga Choo Choo," his first to sell over one million copies, for which the RCA Victor Company awarded him a gold pressing of the selection. By the end of 1940, the juke boxes were attracting $150,000,000.00

yearly; it was estimated that one in every four of these nickels went to play a Miller recording.

1941 heard Hollywood calling, so Glenn took the Orchestra to the coast to make the very popular "Sun Valley Serenade" for 20th Century Fox. Becoming fond of the coast Glenn bought an orange ranch which he called "Tuxedo Junction" in memory of his famous recording of the piece. Late in this year Glenn started his weekly non-commercial show on Mutual called "Sunset Serenade." Each week he played the five tunes chosen by servicemen as their favourites; he also donated three radio-phonographs with recordings to a service centre or hospital each week.

Early in 1942 he made his second and last film "Orchestra Wives," which portrayed very accurately the behind-the-scenes activity of a band on tour. This was followed in September by Glenn's acceptance of a commision in the USAAF. Exempt from the draft, being overage, Glenn offered the following public statement as explanation:

"I, like every American, have an obligation to fulfill. That obligation is to lend as much support as I can to winning this war. It is not enough for me to sit back and buy bonds . . . . I sincerely feel that I owe a debt of gratitude to my country . . . . . I am sure that no matter what my career or livelihood would have been, the mere fact that I have had the privilege of exercising the rights to live and work as a free man puts me in the same position as every man in uniform, for it was the freedom and democratic way of life we have, that enabled me to make strides in the right direction."

The band gave its last performance on September 29, 1942, in the Central Theatre in Passaic, New Jersey.

Early in November Captain Glenn Miller arrived in Atlantic City, where, after a lengthy period, he set to work building orchestras for the AAF. Not until July 17, 1943, did the "I Sustain the Wings" show unfold to the world Captain Glenn Miller and his Orchestra of the USAAF. The orchestra, with its string section, Ray McKinley, Mel Powell, Tony Martin, the Crew Chiefs, and, of course, the high standard which was the by-word of the civilian orchestra soon made the programme the most popular on the air.

On June 22, 1944, the huge orchestra which Glenn called a "Hunk of Home" left the States, arriving at Euston Station in London, England, one week later. A scant six months later, word reached America that the band was to cross the channel to entertain troops near the front line, and that Major Glenn Miller, who had flown ahead, had disappeared without a trace.

His A.G.O. File in Washington states,

"MISSING IN FLIGHT — PRESUMED TO BE DEAD."

SECTION II

GLENN MILLER, TROMBONIST, 1925-1937

NOVEMBER 1925

Glenn Miller joins Ben Pollack's Orchestra in Los Angeles, California.

SPRING 1926 BEN POLLACK and his ORCHESTRA

TB Glenn Miller
TP Harry Greenberg, Al Harris;
S Benny Goodman, Clt and AS; Gil Rodin AS; Fud Livingston TS;
Rh Wayne Allen P; Harry Goodman Tu & B; Lou Kestler BJ; Ben Pollack D.

From a photograph courtesy of the Southmore Hotel, Chicago.

14 SEPTEMBER 1926 BEN POLLACK and his ORCHESTRA

TB Glenn Miller;
TP Harry Greenberg, Al Harris;
S Benny Goodman, Clt & AS; Gil Rodin AS; Fud Livingston TS;
Rh Vic Breidis P; Harry Goodman B; Lou "Tiny" Kestler Bj; Ben Pollack D;
VR Ben Pollack, Joey Ray.

36237	**I'd love to call you sweetheart**	Vi Unissued.	
36238	**Sunday**	Vi Unissued.	

9 DECEMBER 1926 BEN POLLACK and his ORCHESTRA

To the personnel of 14 September 1926 *Add* Victor Young, Al Beller, Vln.

37218	**When I first met Mary.** VR, JR.	**Vi 20394.**	
37219	**'Deed I do.** VR, BP.	**Vi 20408,**	HMV BD-5281

17 DECEMBER 1926 BEN POLLACK and his ORCHESTRA

To the personnel of 14 September 1926—*Add* Ilomay Bailey, Williams Sisters VR.

37260	**You're the one for me.** VR, IB.	**Vi 20461.**	
37261	**He's the last word.** VR, WS.	**Vi 20425,**	Vi LX 3003.

24 JUNE 1927 BEN POLLACK and his ORCHESTRA

Same personnel as that of 17 December, 1926.

39058	**That's what you think**	Vi Unissued.	
39059	**Who is your Baby**	Vi Unissued.	

7 JULY 1927 BEN POLLACK and his ORCHESTRA

Same personnel as that of 17 December, 1926.

39090	**Honey Do**	Vi Unissued.	
39091	**I ain't that kind of Baby**	Vi Unissued.	

7 DECEMBER 1927 BEN POLLACK and his ORCHESTRA

TB Glenn Miller;
C Jimmy McPartland, Frank Quartell;
S Benny Goodman Clt; Gil Rodin AS; Larry Binyon TS;
Rh Vic Breidis P; Harry Goodman B; Dick Morgan Bj; Ben Pollack D.

41342	**Waitin' for Katie.** VR, Duet.	**V21184,**	Vi LX 3003.
41343	**Memphis Blues**	**Vi 21185,**	Vi LX 3003.
41344	**California Medley**	Vi Unissued.	

23 JANUARY 1928—Chicago

BENNY GOODMAN and his ORCHESTRA

TB Glenn Miller
C Jimmy McPartland;
Clt Benny Goodman;
Rh Vic Breidis P; Harry Goodman B; Dick Morgan G; Bob Conselmann D

1652 **A Jazz Holiday** **Vo 15656,** (and Vibes.
Br 80027, Br BL-58015.
1653 **A Jazz Holiday** Vo Unissued.
1654 **The Wolverine Blues** **Vo 15656,**
Br 80027, Br BL-58015, HRS 7.
1655 **The Wolverine Blues** Vo Unissued.

21 MARCH 1928 ALL STAR ORCHESTRA

TB Glenn Miller, Tommy Dorsey;
C Jimmy McPartland; Others Unknown;
S Fud Livingston Clt, TS; a; Others unknown;
Rh Joe Tarto Tu; Chauncey Morehouse D; Others unknown;
Vln Joe Venuti; Others unknown;
VR Scrappy Lambert.

43384 **I'm more than satisfied** **Vi 21605**
43385 **Oh Baby!** **Vi 21423.**

6 APRIL 1928 BEN POLLACK and his ORCHESTRA

TB Glenn Miller;
C Jimmy McPartland, Al Harris;
S Benny Goodman Clt; Gil Rodin AS; Bud Freeman TS;
Rh Vic Breidis P; Dick Morgan Bj; Ben Pollack D;
Vln Victor Young, Al Beller.

43540 **Singapore Sorrows.** VR, BP. Vi Scrapped.
43541 **Sweet Sue** **Vi 21437.**

26/28 APRIL 1928 BEN POLLACK and his ORCHESTRA

Same personnel as that of 6 April 1928.

43540 **Singapore Sorrows.** VR, BP. **Vi 21437,**
(2, 3, 4) All 3 takes on:— Vi LX 3003.

1 MAY 1928 ALL STAR ORCHESTRA

To the personnel of 21 March 1928.
Replace Scrappy Lambert, VR, by Gene Austin, VR.

43688 **Add a little wiggle** **Vi 21423.**
43689 **Alexander's Rag Time Band.** VR, GA. Vi Unissued.

4 JUNE 1928—New York

BENNY GOODMAN and his BOYS

TB Glenn Miller;
C Jimmy McPartland;
S Benny Goodman Clt; Fred (Fud) Livingston AS & TS;
Rh Vic Breidis P; Harry Goodman G; Ben Pollack D.

27638 **Jungle Blues.** Clt & TP, BG. **Br 4013,**
Br 80029, Br BL-58015, Br F 500201, BrG A-7839.
27639-1 **Room 1411.** Clt & BS, BG. **Br 4013,**
Br 80029, Br BL-58015, BrG A-7839.
27639-2 **Room 1411.** Clt & BS, BG. **BrF 500201.**
27640 **Blue.** AS & BS, BG. **Br 3975,**
Br 80030, Br BL-58015, BrF 500202, BrG A-7815.
27641 **Shirt Tail Stomp** **Br 3975,**
Br 80030, Br BL-58015, BrF 500202, BrG A-7815.

9 August 1928 NAT SHILKRET directing ALL STAR ORCHESTRA

Personnel is probably the same as that of 21 March 1928, except that the vocalist Scrappy Lambert is replaced by Johnny Marvin.

46354 **There's a Rainbow 'round my shoulder.** **Vi 21667,** HMV B-5584.
46355 **She didn't say Yes.** VR, JM. **Vi 21667.**
46356 **My Dream Melody** **Vi 22054.**
46357 **Waiting at the end of the road** **Vi 22073.**

26 January 1929 GROUP from the DORSEY BROTHERS' ORCH.

TB Glenn Miller TB & a; Tommy Dorsey;
TP Fuzzy Farrar, Leo McConville, Phil Napoleon;
S Jimmy Dorsey, Arnold Brilhart, Herbie Spencer;
Tu Hank Stern;
Rh Arthur Schutt P; Joe Tarto B; Eddie Lang G; Unknown Bj; Stan King D.
Vln Unknown;
VR Smith Ballew, Bing Crosby.

401560 **The Spell of the Blues.** a, GM. **OK 41181,** PaE R-385.
401561 **Let's do it again.** VR, BC. **OK 41181,** PaE R-331.
401562 **My kinda love.** VR, BC; a, GM. **OK 41188,** PaE R-374, PaE R-2475.

15 March 1929 GROUP from the DORSEY BROTHERS' ORCH.

Same personnel as that of 26 January 1929.

401715 **Mean to Me.** VR, SB; a, GM. **OK 41210,** OdF 165685, PaE R-374.
401716 **Button up your overcoat.** a, GM. **OK 41210,** OdF 165685, PaE R-391.
401717 **I'll never ask for more.** VR, SB. **OK 41220,** Ar 4424, OdF 165765, PaE E-6179.

3 April 1929 DORSEY BROTHERS' ORCHESTRA

TB Glenn Miller; Tommy Dorsey;
TP Fuzzy Farrar, Leo McConville, Phil Napoleon;
S Jimmy Dorsey, Arnold Brilhart, Jim Crosson;
Rh Arthur Schutt P; Joe Tarto Tu; Eddie Lang G; Chauncey Morehouse D;
St Murphy Kellner, Sam Rates, Nat Brusilhoft Vln; Emil Stark Cello;
W Irving Kohn Oboe; Phil Raines Bassoon;
VR Smith Ballew.

401775/6 **Lover come back to me.** VR, SB. **OK 41223,** PaE R-391

18/19 April 1929 RED NICHOLS and his ORCHESTRA

Note:—Br 6800 series are labelled "Red Nichols and his 5 Pennies"

TB Glenn Miller, Jack Teagarden;
TP Red Nichols, Leo McConville;
S Benny Goodman Clt; Babe Russin TS;
Rh Jack Russin P; Carl Kress G; Gene Krupa D;
VR Scrappy Lambert.

E29708 **Indiana.** (Several Takes Used) **Br 4286,** Br 4373, Br 6824, Br 80006, BrE 3960, BrE 01853, BrF 1002, BrG 8264, BrE 01591, Vo 4500.
E29709 **Dinah.** **Br 4286** Br 4373, Br 6824, Br 80006, BrE 3960, BrE 01853, BrE 01591, BrF 1002, BrG 8264, Vo 4500.
E29710 **On the Alamo** (Several Takes Used) **Br 4363,** Br 6825, BrE 5019, BrE 01586, BrF 1029, BrF 500403, BrG 8265.

20 MAY 1929 RED NICHOLS and his ORCHESTRA

TB Glenn Miller, Jack Teagarden;
TP Red Nichols, Leo McConville;
S Jimmy Dorsey Clt & AS; Larry Binyon TS & F;
Rh Arthur Schutt P; Carl Kress G; Gene Krupa D;
St Ed Bergman, Al Beller Vln; Bill Schumann Cello & Oboe;
VR Jack Teagarden, Scrappy Lambert.

E29957 **Sally, won't you come back.** (12-in.) **Br 20092,** BrE 101

7 JUNE 1929 RED NICHOLS and his ORCHESTRA

Same personnel as that of 20 May 1929.

E 29994 **It had to be you.** (12-in.) **Br 20092,** BrE 101
E 29995 **I'll see you in my dreams.** (12-in) **Br 20091.**
E 29996 **Some of these days.** (12-in.) **Br 20091.**

12 JUNE 1929 RED NICHOLS and his ORCHESTRA

TB Glenn Miller, Jack Teagarden;
TP Red Nichols, Leo McConville;
S Pee Wee Russell Clt; Bud Freeman TS;
Rh Jack Russin P; Art Miller B; Eddie Condon Bj; Dave Tough D;
VR Red McKenzie.

E 30056 **Who Cares** **Br 4778,** Br 6831.
E 30057 **Rose of Washington Square** **Br 4778,** Br 6831, BrE 1204.

20 AUGUST 1929 RED NICHOLS and his ORCHESTRA

TB Glenn Miller, Jack Teagarden;
TP Red Nichols, Leo McConville;
S Benny Goodman Clt; Fud Livingston TS; Jimmy Dorsey AS; Harry Goodman Tu;
Rh Jack Russin P; Art Miller B; Eddie Condon Bj; Dave Tough D;
St Ed Bergman, Al Beller Vln; Bill Schumann Cello & Oboe;
VR Scrappy Lambert, Red McKenzie.

30502/3 **I may be wrong.** VR, SL. **Br 4500.**
30504/5 **The New Yorker.** VR, RM. **Br 4500.**

23 AUGUST 1929 NAT SHILKRET directing HOUSE BAND

To the personnel of 9 August 1928—*Add* Frank Mann VR.

55653 **Too wonderful for words.** VR, FM. **Vi 22104** HMV 5718
55654 **You made me love you** Vi Unissued.
55655 **Steppin' Along** **Vi 22104,** HMV 5718.

9 SEPTEMBER 1929 RED NICHOLS and his ORCHESTRA

TB Glenn Miller, Jack Teagarden;
TP Red Nichols, Leo McConville;
S Benny Goodman Clt; Jimmy Dorsey Clt & AS;
Rh Jack Russin P; Art Miller B; Teg Brown Bj; Dave Tough D.

E 30538/39G **Nobody Knows** **Br 4790,** Br 6832, BrE 02505, BrF 8744, BrG A-8744.
E 30540/41G **Smiles** **Br 4790,** Br 6832, BrE 02505, BrF 8744, BrG A-8744.
E 30542/43G **Say it with Music** Br Unissued (Rejected)

10 SEPTEMBER 1929 LOUISIANA RHYTHM KINGS

TB Glenn Miller;
TP Red Nichols;
S Jimmy Dorsey Clt & AS;
Rh Jack Russin P; Eddie Condon G; Dave Tough D.

E 30544 **Waiting at the end of the road** **Vo 15833.**
E 30545 **Little by little** **Vo 15841.**
E 30546 **Marianne** **Vo 15833.**

8 NOVEMBER 1929 NAT SHILKRET directing HOUSE BAND

Personnel is the same as that of 9 August 1928.

57532 **I'll close my eyes to the rest** **Vi 22197**
57533 **Deep in the arms of love** **Vi 22197**

14 NOVEMBER 1929—New York

MOUND CITY BLUE BLOWER

TB Glenn Miller;
Comb Red McKenzie;
S "Pee Wee" Russell Clt; Coleman Hawkins TS;
Rh Al Morgan B; Jack Bland G; Eddie Condon Bj; Gene Krupa D.

57145 **Hello Lola** **Vi 38100,**
BB 6720, BB 10037, GrF K-6501, GrF K-8525, HMV BD 6150, HMV B 8952, HMV JO 149, HMVSw JK 2260, HMV 7EG8096.

57146 **One Hour** **Vi 38100,**
BB 10037, GrF K-6501, GrF 8525, HMV BD 6163, HMV B 8952, HMV JO 149, HMVSw JK-2260, HMV 7EG8096.

20 JANUARY 1930 LOUISIANA RHYTHM KINGS

TB Glenn Miller;
TP Red Nichols;
S Jimmy Dorsey Clt & AS; Adrian Rollini BS; Babe Russin TS;
Rh Jack Russin P; Eddie Condon G; Gene Krupa D.

E 31943 **Swanee** **Br 4845,**
Br 6834, BrF 500325.
E 31944 **Squeeze Me** **Br 4953,** BrE 03282.
E 31945 **Oh, Lady be good.** **Br 4706,**
Br 6829, BrE 02676, BrE 03324, BrG A-8687..
E 31946 **Sweet Sue** **Br 4953,** BrE 03282.
E 31947 **Meanest kind of Blues** **Br 4845,**
Br 6734, BrE 03324, BrG A-8687.
E 31948 **I have to have you** **Br 4706,**
Br 6829, BrE 02676.

27 JANUARY 1930 LOUISIANA RHYTHM KINGS

Same personnel as that of 20 January 1930.

E 31911 **Over the Billowy Sea** **Br 4908,** Br 6837.
E 31912 **Lazy Daddy** **Br 4923** Br 6838.
E 31913 **Caravan** **Br 4908,** Br 6837.
E 31914 **Pretty Baby** **Br 4938,** Br 6840.
E 31915 **Tell Me** **Br 4938,**
Br 6840, BrF 500325.
E 31916 **There's Egypt in your dreamy eyes** **Br 4923** Br 6838.

3 February 1930 RED NICHOLS and his ORCHESTRA

TB Glenn Miller, Jack Teagarden;
TP Red Nichols, Ruby Weinstein;
S Jimmy Dorsey Clt & AS; Adrian Rollini BS; Babe Russin TS;
Rh Jack Russin P; Teg Brown G; Gene Krupa D.

E 31923 **I'm just wild about Harry** **Br 4839,**
Br 6833, BrE 1121, BrF 500405.
E 31924 **After you've gone** **Br 4839,**
Br 6833, BrE 1104, BrF 500405.

14 February 1930 RED NICHOLS and his ORCHESTRA

Same personnel as that of 3 February 1930.
E 32040 **I want to be happy** **Br 4724,**
Br 6830, Br 80007, BrE 1032, BrF 8832, BrG 8832.
E 32041 **Tea for Two** **Br 4724,**
Br 6830, Br 80007, BrE 1032, BrF 8832, BrG 8832.

2 July 1930 RED NICHOLS and his ORCHESTRA

TB Glenn Miller, Jack Teagarden;
TP Red Nichols, Ruby Weinstein, Charlie Teagarden;
S Benny Goodman Clt; Sid Stoneman AS; Babe Russin TS;
Rh Joe Sullivan P; Art Miller B; Teg Brown G; Gene Krupa D.

E 33304 **Peg o' my heart** (Several takes used) **Br 4877,**
Br 6835, Br 80004, BrE 1019, BrF 8962, BrG 8962.
E 33305 **Sweet Georgia Brown** **Br 4944,**
Br 6841, BrE 1048.
E 33306 **China Boy** (Several takes used) **Br 4877,**
Br 6835, Br 80004, BrE 1019, BrF 8962, BrG 8962.
E 33307 **Chong, he come from** Br Unissued (reject)

3 July 1930 RED NICHOLS and his ORCHESTRA

Same personnel as that of 2 July 1930.
E 33333 **Sheik of Araby** **Br 4885**
Br 6836, Br 80005, BrE 1104, BrF 500403, BrG 68868.
E 33334 **Shim-Me-Sha-Wobble** **Br 4885,**
Br 6836, Br 80005, BrE 1204, BrF 500403, BrG 68868.

27 August 1930 RED NICHOLS and his ORCHESTRA

TB Glenn Miller, Jack Teagarden;
TP Red Nichols, Charlie Teagarden;
S Benny Goodman Clt; Bud Freeman TS; Adrian Rollini BS;
Rh Joe Sullivan P; Art Miller B; Teg Brown G; Gene Krupa D.

E 34109 **Carolina in the morning** **Br 4925,**
Br 6839, BrE 1062.
E 34110 **How come you do me** Br Unissued (Reject)
E 34111 **Who** **Br 4925**
Br 6839, BrE 1062.
E 34112 **By the Shalimar** **Br 4944,**
Br 6841, BrE 1048.

26 SEPTEMBER 1930 RED NICHOLS and his ORCHESTRA

To the personnel of 27 August 1930:
Replace Bud Freeman TS; by Babe Russin TS.
Joe Sullivan P; by Jack Russin P.

E 34626 **On Revival Day**—Part 1. Br Unissued (Reject)
E 34627 **On Revival Day**—Part 1. **Br 6026,** Br 6843, BrE 1087.
E 34628 **On Revival Day**—Part 2 **Br 6026,** Br 6843, BrE 1087.

23 OCTOBER 1930 RED NICHOLS and his ORCHESTRA

TB Glenn Miller, Jack Teagarden;
TP Red Nichols, Charlie Teagarden, Ruby Weinstein;
S Benny Goodman Clt; Larry Binyon TS; Sid Stoneburn AS; A. Rollini BS;
Rh Jack Russin P; Art Miller B; Teg Brown G; Gene Krupa; D.
Vln Ed Bergman, Ed Solinski;
VR Dick Robertson.

E 34958 **Embraceable You** **Br 4957,** Br 6842, BrF 9008, BrG 9008.
E 34959 **I Got Rhythm** **Br 4957,** Br 6842, BrE 1300, BrF 9008, BrG 9008.
E 34960 **A Girl Friend of a Boy Friend** **Me M-12005.**
E 34961 **Sweet Jeannie Lee.** **Me M-12005,Pana 25001.**

6 NOVEMBER 1930 RED NICHOLS and his ORCHESTRA

To the personnel of 23 October 1930 *Add*—Harold Arlen VR.

E 35214 **Linda.** VR, HA. **Br 4982,** Br 6844, BrF 9003, BrG 9003.
E 35215 **Yours and Mine** **Br 4982,** Br 6844, BrF 9003, BrG 9003.

7 NOVEMBER 1930 THE TRAVELLERS (A Dorsey Brothers' Group)

TB Glenn Miller, Tommy Dorsey;
TP Charlie Marqualies, Lou Garcia, William Moore;
S Jimmy Dorsey, Arnold Brilhart, Bud Freeman;
Rh Arthur Schutt P; Hank Stern B; Eddie Lang G; Stanley King D;
VR Wesley Vaughn.

404543/100434 **Can't this be love** **Ha 1242,** Cl 5117, Po 34152.
404544/100452 **Fine and Dandy** **Ha 1260,** OK 41471, PaE R-993, Po 34153.
404545 **But I can't make a man.** a, GM. **Ha 1260,** OK 41471, PaE R-882, Po 34152.

7 NOVEMBER 1930 BENNY GOODMAN and his ORCHESTRA

These recordings are very commercial. They contain choruses by the men listed, but the total personnel is unknown.

TB Glenn Miller, Jack Teagarden;
S Benny Goodman Clt; Sid Stoneburn AS; Larry Binyon TS;
G Eddie Lang.

E 35341 **He's not worth your tears** **Me M-12023.**
E 35342 **Linda** **Me M-12024.**
E 35343 **And when your lips meet mine** **Me M-12023.**
E 35344 **Overnight** **Me M-12024.**

1 DECEMBER 1930 RED NICHOLS and his ORCHESTRA

TB Glenn Miller;
TP Red Nichols, Charlie Teagarden, Wingy Mannone;
S Jimmy Dorsey Clt & AS; Babe Russin TS;
Rh Joe Sullivan P; Art Miller B; Gene Krupa D;

E 35618 **My Honey's lovin' arms.** **Br 6012,**
BrE 1121, BrF 9005, BrG 9005.
E 35619 **Rockin' Chair.** VR, W. Mannone. **Br 6012,**
BrE 01852, BrF 9005, BrG 9005.

10 DECEMBER 1930 RED NICHOLS and his ORCHESTRA

TB Glenn Miller;
TP Red Nichols, Charlie Teagarden, Wingy Mannone;
S Benny Goodman, Clt & BS; Babe Russin TS;
Rh Jack Russin P; Art Miller B; Gene Krupa D.

E 35733 **Bug-a-Boo.** VR, W. Mannone. **Br 6058,**
BrE 1120, Me M-12495, Pe 15684, Ro 1950.
E 35734 **Corrine Corrina.** VR, W. Mannone. **Br 6058,**
BrE 1120, BrF 9024, BrG 9024, Me M-12495, Pe 15684, Ro 1950.
E 35735 **How come you like me like you do** **Br 6149,** BrE 1180.

14 JANUARY 1931 BENNY GOODMAN and his ORCHESTRA

Same personnel as that of 7 November 1930.

E 35156 **I'm happy when you're happy** **Me M-12090.**
E 35157 **You didn't have to tell me** **Me M-12090.**
E 35158 **Falling in love again** **Me M-12079.**
E 35924 **If you haven't got a girl** **Me M-12079.**

16 JANUARY 1931 RED NICHOLS and his ORCHESTRA

Same personnel as that of 23 October 1930.

E 35167 **You said it** **Br 6029,**
Br 6711, Br 6842.
E 35168 **Sweet and hot** **Br 6029,**
Br 6711, BrE 1300.
E 35169 **Keep a Song** Br Unissued (Reject)

5 FEBRUARY 1931 BENNY GOODMAN and his ORCHESTRA

Same personnel as that of 7 November 1930.

E 35834 **We can live on love** **Me M-12120.**
E 35835 **When your lover has gone** **Me M-12120.**
E 35836 **99 out of every 100 want to be loved** **Me M-12100,** Panna 25013
E 35837 **Mine yesterday, his today** **Me M-12100.**

7 FEBRUARY 1931 JOHNNY WALKER and his ORCHESTRA

TB Glenn Miller TB & a; Jack Teagarden TB & VR;
TP Ruby Weinstein, Charlie Teagarden;
S Benny Goodman Clt; Sid Stoneburn AS; Larry Binyon TS;
Rh Arthur Schutt P; Harry Goodman B; Dick McDonough G; Gene Krupa D.

151290 **When your lover has gone** **Co 240-D.**
151291 **Walkin' my baby back home** **Co 240-D.**

19 FEBRUARY 1931 THE CHARLESTON CHASERS

TB Glenn Miller, Jack Teagarden;
TP Charlie Teagarden, Ruby Weinstein;
S Benny Goodman Clt; Sid Stoneburn AS; Larry Binyon TS;
Rh Arthur Schutt P; Harry Goodman B; Dick McDonough G; Gene Krupa D.

151292 **Basin Street Blues.** a, GM. **Co 2415-D.**
Bi 1098, Br 7645, Co 2914-D, HJCA 89, Od 2307, OK 41577, PaE R-1356, PaE DP 377.

151293 **Beale Street Blues.** a, GM. **Co 2415-D.**
Bi 1098, Br 7645, Co 2914-D, HJCA 89, OK 41577, PaE R-1413.

19 FEBRUARY 1931 RED NICHOLS and his ORCHESTRA

Same personnel as that of 23 October 1930.

E 36108 **Things I never knew till now** **Br 6068.**
E 36109 **Teardrops and Kisses** **Br 6070.**
E 36110 **You were sincere** **Br 6070.**
E 36111 **Keep a song in your heart** **Br 6068.**

26 FEBRUARY 1931 THE TRAVELLERS

Personnel unknown except for:
TB Glenn Miller, Tommy Dorsey

E 36186 **You Said It** **Me M-12113.**
E 36187 **Sweet and Hot** **Me M-12113.**
E 36188 **I've got a sweet someone** **Me M-12148.**
E 36189 **Dream a little Dream** **Me M-12148.**

18 MARCH 1931 BENNY GOODMAN and his ORCHESTRA

Same personnel as that of 7 November 1930.

E 36181 **What have I got to do tonight?** **Me M-12131,** Pana 25046.
E 36182 **Little Joe** **Me M-12149.**
E 36183 **It looks like love** **Me M-12149.**
E 36184 **I wanna be around my Baby** **Me M-12131.**

24 APRIL 1931 RED NICHOLS and his ORCHESTRA

TB Glenn Miller, George Still;
TP Red Nichols, Ruby Weinstein, Charlie Teagarden;
S Benny Goodman, Clt; Sid Stoneburn AS; Larry Binyon TS;
Rh Fulton McGrath P; Art Miller B; Teg Brown G; Gene Krupa D;
Vln Ed Bergman, Ed Solinski.

E 36728 **It's the Darndest Thing** **Br 6191,** BrE 1275.
E 36729 **Singing the Blues** **Br 6191,** BrE 1275.
E 36730 **Love is like that** **Br 6118.**

26 MAY 1931 RED NICHOLS and his ORCHESTRA

TB Glenn Miller;
TP Red Nichols;
S Jimmy Dorsey Clt & AS; Babe Russin TS;
Rh Jack Russin P; Art Miller B; Perry Botkin G; Gene Krupa D;
VR Red McKenzie.

E 36830 **Just a Crazy Song** **Br 6133,**
BrE 1163, BrF 9090, BrG 9090.

E 36831 **You Rascal You.** VR, RM. **Br 6133,**
BrE 1163, BrF 9090, BrG 9090.

E 36832 **Moan You Moaners** **Br 6149,**
BrE 1180, BrF 9099, BrG 9099.

11 JUNE 1931 RED NICHOLS and his ORCHESTRA

Same personnel as that of 26 May 1931.

E 36855 **Slow But Sure** **Br 6138,**
BrF 9094, BrG 9094.

E 36856 **Little Girl** **Br 6138,**
BrF 9094, BrG 9094.

E 36857 **How Time Can Fly** **Br 6164.**

20 JUNE 1931 BENNY GOODMAN and his ORCHESTRA

Same personnel as that of 7 November 1930.

E 36835 **Slow But Sure** **Me M-12205.**

E 36874 **Pardon Me My Pretty Baby** **Me M-11208,**
May 2030, Pana 25069.

E 36875 **What am I going to do for loving** **Me M-11208,**
May 2030, Pana 25069.

E 36876 **You can't stop me from loving you** **Me M-12205.**

24 JUNE 1931 RED NICHOLS and his ORCHESTRA

Same personnel as that of 26 May 1931.

E 36877 **How long, how long Blues** **Br 6160,**
BrE 1213, BrF 9117, BrG 9117.

E 36878 **Fan It** **Br 6160,**
BrE 1213, BrF 9117, BrG 9117.

30 JULY 1931 THE TRAVELLERS

Personnel unknown except for:
TB Glenn Miller, Tommy Dorsey;

E 36946 **I can't get Mississippi off my mind** **Me M-12230.**

E 36947 **I Apologize** **Me M-12227.**

E 36948 **Beggin' for Love** **Me M-12227**, BrE 01224.

8 APRIL 1933 MILDRED BAILEY and the DORSEY BROTHERS ORCHESTRA

TB Glenn Miller, Tommy Dorsey;
TP Bunny Berigan;
S Jimmy Dorsey Clt & AS; Larry Binyon TS;
Rh Fulton McGrath P; Artie Bernstein B; Dick McDonough G; Stan King D;
a Glenn Miller, Herbie Spencer.

13208 **Is That Religion.** VR, M.B a GM. **Br 6558,**
BrE 01544, BrF 500269.

13209 **Harlem Lullaby.** VR, MB. **Br 6558,**
BrE 01544, BrF 500269.

6 JUNE 1933 MILDRED BAILEY and the DORSEY BROTHERS' ORCHESTRA

Same personnel as that of 8 April 1933.

13427 **There's a cabin in the pines.** VR, MB **Br 6587**
BrE 01564, BrF 500305.

13428 **Lazy Bones.** VR, MB. **Br 6587,**
BrE 01564, BrF 500305.

5 SEPTEMBER 1933 MILDRED BAILEY and the DORSEY BROTHERS' ORCHESTRA

Same personnel as that of 8 April 1933.

13955 **Shouting the Amen Chorus.** VR, MB **Br 6655,** BrE 01593, BrF 500335.

13956 **Snowball.** VR, MB. **Br 6655,** BrE 01593, BrF 500335.

17 OCTOBER 1933 MILDRED BAILEY and the DORSEY BROTHERS' ORCHESTRA

To the personnel of 8 April 1933 *Add*—Manny Klein TP.

14159 **Give me liberty or give me love** VR, MB. **Br 6680,** BrE 01631, BrF 9500, BrG 9500.

14160 **Doin' the Uptown, Downtown.** VR, MB. **Br 6680,** BrE 01631, BrF 9500, BrG 9500.

23 APRIL 1934 DORSEY BROTHERS' ORCHESTRA

TB Glenn Miller, Tommy Dorsey, Chuck Campbell;
TP Manny Klein;
S Larry Binyon, Jimmy Dorsey, Paul Hamilton;
Rh Fulton McGrath P; Artie Bernstein B; Dick McDonough G; Stan King D;
VR Kay Weber, Bob Snyder.

Note:—The name in brackets is the name of the orchestra on the labels.

15090 **How do I know.** VR, KW. (Paul Hamilton) **Vo 2708.**
15091 **Judy.** (Dorsey Brothers) **Br 6938,** BrE 02006.
15092 **May I.** (Bob Snyder) **Vo 2707.**
15093 **Love Thy Neighbour.** (Bob Snyder) **Vo 2707.**
15094 **I've had my moments** (Paul Hamilton) **Vo 2708.**

21 MAY 1934 DORSEY BROTHERS' ORCHESTRA

TB Glenn Miller, Tommy Dorsey;
TP Manny Klein, Bob Snyder;
S Jimmy Dorsey, Larry Binyon, Paul Hamilton;
Rh Fulton McGrath P; Artie Bernstein B; Dick McDonough G; Stan King D;
VR Kay Weber, Bob Snyder, Smith Ballew.

Note:—The name in brackets is the name of the orchestra on the labels.

15246 **On Accounta I Love You.** VR, SB. (Smith Ballew) **Ro 2886,** Ba 33078, Me M-13042, Or 2912, Pe 15945.
15247 **So Help Me.** (P. Hamilton) **Vo 2721.**
15248 **Easy Come, Easy Go.** (P. Hamilton) **Vo 2721.**
15249-1 **Annie's Cousin Fanny.** a GM. (D. Brothers) Br Unissued (Reject).

4 JUNE 1934 DORSEY BROTHERS' ORCHESTRA

Same personnel as that of 21 May 1934.

15249-2 **Annie's Cousin Fanny.** a GM. **Br 6938.**

14 August 1934 DORSEY BROTHERS' ORCHESTRA

TB Glenn Miller, Tommy Dorsey, Don Mattison;
TP George Throw *or* Jerry Neary;
S Jimmy Dorsey Clt & AS; Jack Stacey, Skeets Herfurt TS;
Rh Bob Van Epps P; Delmar Kaplan B; Roc Hillman G; Ray McKinley D;
VR Bob Crosby, Kay Weber.

38301 **Heat Wave** **De 208**
38302 **By Heck** **De 118.**
38303 **Stop, Look and Listen** **De 208.**
38304 **I'm Getting Sentimental Over You.**
VR, BC. **De 115,** De 3942, BrE 02573

15 August 1934 DORSEY BROTHERS' ORCHESTRA

Same personnel as that of 14 August 1934.

38307 **Long May We Live** **De 115.**
38308 **Annie's Cousin Fanny.** a GM. **De 117.**
38309 **Doctor Heckle and Mister Jibe** **De 117.**

23 August 1934 DORSEY BROTHERS' ORCHESTRA

Same personnel as that of 14 August 1934.

38407 **Milenberg Joys** **De 119,** BrE 02023.
38408 **St. Louis Blues.** **De 119,** De 3524,
Br E01892
38409 **Honeysuckle Rose**—Part 1. VR, Trio **De 296,** BrE 01890.
38410 **Honeysuckle Rose**—Part 2. VR, Trio **De 296,** BrE 01890.
38411-A/B **Sand Man** De Unissued.
38412 **Basin Street Blues.** VR, BC. **De 118,** BrE01892.

30 August 1934 DORSEY BROTHERS' ORCHESTRA

Same personnel as that of 14 August 1934.

38485 **I Ain't Gonna Sin No More** **De 116.**
38486 **I Can't Dance** **De 116.**

21 September 1934 DORSEY BROTHERS' ORCHESTRA

Same personnel as that of 14 August 1934.

38705 **Lost in a Fog** **De 195.**
38706 **Mama, Yo Quiero Un Novio** De Unissued
38707-A/B/C—**The Moon Was Yellow** De Unissued
38708 **I Couldn't Be Mean To You** **De 195.**
38709 **How Can You Face Me** **De 196**

23 September 1934 DORSEY BROTHERS' ORCHESTRA

Same personnel as that of 14 August 1934.

38719 **Don't Let It Bother You** **De 207.**
38720 **The Breeze** **De 207.**
38721 **Out in the Cold Again** **De 206.**
38722 **Day Dreaming** **De 206.**

28 September 1934 DORSEY BROTHERS' ORCHESTRA

Same personnel as that of 14 August 1934

38707-D **The Moon Was Yellow** **De 196.**
38754 **Okay Toots** **De 259.**
38755 **Careful of the Music** **De 258.**
38756 **When My Ship Comes In** **De 259.**
38757 **With Your Head On My Shoulder** **De 258.**
38758 **Missouri Misery** **De 297**

24 October 1934 DORSEY BROTHERS' ORCHESTRA

Same personnel as that of 14 August 1934.

38883-A/B	**Fun to be Fooled**	De Unissued
38884	**Let's Walk Around the Block**	**De 260.**

29 October 1934 DORSEY BROTHERS' ORCHESTRA

Same personnel as that of 14 August 1934.

38914	**What a Difference a Day Made**	**De 283.**
38919	**Dream Man**	**De 291.**
38920	**What Can I Say in a Love Song**	**De 283.**

7 November 1934 DORSEY BROTHERS' ORCHESTRA

Same personnel as that of 14 August 1934.

38883-C	**Fun to be Fooled**	**De 260.**
38963	**Hands Across the Table**	**De 291.**
38964	**Love is Just Around the Corner**	**De 311.**
38965	**Here is My Heart**	**De 311.**

15 November 1934 DORSEY BROTHERS' ORCHESTRA

Same personnel as that of 14 August 1934.

38411-C	**Sand Man**	**De 297.**
39020	**Apache**	**De 314.**
39021	**It's Dark on Observatory Hill**	**De 314.**
39022	**Blame it on My Youth**	**De 320.**

20 November 1934 FRANKIE TRUMBAUER and his ORCHESTRA

TB Glenn Miller;
TP Nat Natoli, Bunny Berigan;
S Artie Shaw Clt & AS; Frank Trumbauer, Jack Shore AS; Larry Binyon TS;
Rh Roy Bargy P; Artie Bernstein B; Lionel Hall G; Jack Williams D.

86219	**Blue Moon.**	**Vi 24812,** HMV BD-119, GrF K-7454.
86220	**Plantation Moods**	**Vi 24834,** HMV X-4454.
86221	**Down to Uncle Bill's**	**Vi 24812,** HMV BD-119, GrF K-7454.
86222	**Troubled**	**Vi 24834,** HMV BD-158, HMV X-4454.

27 November 1934 DORSEY BROTHERS' ORCHESTRA

TB Glenn Miller, Tommy Dorsey, Don Mattison;
TP George Throw;
S Jimmy Dorsey Clt & AS; Jack Stacy, Skeets Herfurt TS;
Rh Bob Van Epps P; Delmar Kaplan B; Roc Hillman G; Ray McKinley D;
VR Kay Weber, Bob Crosby.

39102	**Anything Gives**	**De 318.**
39103	**All Through the Night.**	**De 318.**
39104	**You're Tops**	**De 319.**

30 November 1934 DORSEY BROTHERS' ORCHESTRA

Same personnel as that of 27 November 1934.

39118	**I Get a Kick Out of You**	**De 319.**
39119	**You Didn't Know Me From Adam**	**De 320.**
39120	**If It's Love**	**De 321.**

21 December 1934 DORSEY BROTHERS' ORCHESTRA

Same personnel as that of 27 November 1934.

39181	**I Believe in Miracles**	**De 335**	
39182	**Dancing with my Shadow**	**De 335.**	
39183	**Home Ties**	**De 340.**	
39184	**The Church Bells Toll**	**De 340.**	

28 December 1934 DORSEY BROTHERS' ORCHESTRA

Same personnel as that of 27 November 1934

39210	**Au Revoir L'Amour**	**De 357.**	
39211	**Singing a Happy Song**	**De 357.**	
39212	**I Was Lucky**	**De 358.**	
39213	**Rhythm of the Rain**	**De 358.**	

4 January 1935 DORSEY BROTHERS' ORCHESTRA

Same personnel as that of 27 November 1934

39224	**Night Wind**	**De 376.**	
39225	**I'm Just a Little Boy Blue.**	**De 348.**	
39226	**New Deal in Love**	**De 348.**	

11 January 1935 DORSEY BROTHERS' ORCHESTRA

Same personnel as that of 27 November 1934.

39241	**Dinah.** VR, BC.	**De 376,**	BrE 02573.
39243	**Solitude** (12-in.) VR, BC.	**De 15013,**	BrE 0135,
	DeE K867.		

18 January 1935 DORSEY BROTHERS' ORCHESTRA

Same personnel as that of 27 November 1934.

39264	**Tiny Little Finger Prints**	**De 367.**	
39265	**I'm Facing the Music**	**De 367.**	
39266	**I Threw a Bean Bag at the Moon**	**De 368.**	
39267	**The Farmer Takes a Wife**	**De 368.**	

23 January 1935 DORSEY BROTHERS' ORCHESTRA

Same personnel as that of 27 November 1934.

39278	**Don't be afraid to tell your mother**	**De 371.**	
39280	**Lullaby of the Rain**	**De 370.**	
39281	**The Words in My Heart**	**De 370.**	
39282	**I'm Going Shopping With You**	**De 371**	

6 February 1935 DORSEY BROTHERS' ORCHESTRA

Same personnel as that of 27 November 1934.

39338	**I've Got Your Number**	**De 515.**	
39339	**You're Okay**	**De 1304.**	
39340	**Weary Blues**	**De 469,**	BrE 02149.
39341	**Weary Blues** (12-in.)	**De 15013,**	BrE 0135.
39342	**Tail Spin.**	**De 560,**	De 4204,
	BrE 02023		
39343	**Eccentric**	**De 1304.**	
39344	**Dese, Dem, Dose**	**De 469.**	
39345	**Dippermouth Blues**	**De 561**	
39346	**Tomorrow's Another Day**	**De 515.**	

15 MARCH 1935 CLARK RANDALL'S ORCHESTRA (Bob Crosby Group)

TB Glenn Miller, Artie Foster;
TP Phil Hart, Yank Lawson;
S Matty Matlock Clt & AS; Gil Rodin AS; Eddie Miller, Deane Kincaide TS;
Rh Gil Bowers P; Bob Haggart B; Hilton "Nappy" Lamare G; Ray Bauduc D;
VR Clark Randall, Hilton "Nappy" Lamare.

17047 **Troublesome Trumpet** **Br 7415**
17048 **When Icky Morgan Plays the Organ.** a GM. **Br 7415.**

15 MARCH 1935 GIL RODIN'S ORCHESTRA (Bob Crosby Group)

Same personnel as that of Clark Randall's Orchestra, 15 March 1935.

17049 **What's the Reason** **Pe 16107,** Ba 33410, Cq 8527, Me M-13377, Or 3130, Ro 2504.
17050 **Restless.** VR, CR. **Pe 16107,** Ba 33410, Me M-13377, Or 3130, Ro 2504.

22 MARCH 1935 CLARK RANDALL'S ORCHESTRA (Bob Crosby Group)

Same personnel as that of 15 March 1935.

17160 **Jitterbug.** VR, HL. **Br 7466.**
17161 **If you're looking for someone to love** **Br 7466.**

29 MARCH 1935 CLARK RANDALL'S ORCHESTRA (Bob Crosby Group)

Same personnel as that of 15 March 1935.

17218 **Driftin' Tide.** VR, CR. **Br 7436,**
17219 **Here Comes Your Pappy.** VR, HL. **Br 7436,** Rex 8500.

29 MARCH 1935 GIL RODIN'S ORCHESTRA (Bob Crosby Group)

Same personnel as that of 15 March 1935.

17220 **Right About Face** **Pe 16106,** Ba 33409, Me M-13376, Or 3139, Ro 2503.
17221 **Love's Serenade** **Pe 16106,** Ba 33409, Me M-13376, Or 3139, Ro 2503.

25 APRIL 1935 GLENN MILLER and his ORCHESTRA

Note:—This was a studio recording group only; it is the same session as that on page 22.

TB Glenn Miller, Jack Jenny;
TP Bunny Berigan, Charlie Spivak;
S Johnny Mince Clt & AS; Eddie Miller TS;
Rh Claude Thornhill P; Delmar Kaplan B; Larry Hall G; Ray Bauduc D;
St Harry Bluestone, Vladimir Selinski Vln; Bill Schumann Cello; Harry Waller Vla;
VR Smith Ballew.

17379 **A Blues Serenade.** VR, SB. **Co 3051-D,** Bi 1022.
17380 **Moonlight on the Ganges.** VR, SB. **Co 3051-D,** Bi 1022.
17381 **In a Little Spanish Town** **Co 3058-D,** Bi 1045, Co 35881, CoE FB-1150.

Note:—Jack Jenny TB and the Strings *out*.

17382 **Solo Hop** (Pagan Love Song) **Co 3058-D,** Bi 1045, Co 35881, CoE FB-1150, Epic EG 5700 (Epic issued under B. Berigan's name).

10 May 1935 RAY NOBLE and his ORCHESTRA

TB Glenn Miller, Will Bradley;
TP Charlie Spivak, George "Pee Wee" Erwin;
S "Toots" Mondello, Johnny Mince, Mike Doty, Bud Freeman;
Rh Claude Thornhill P; Delmar Kaplan B; George Van Epps G; Bill Harty D;
Vln Nick Pisanni, Fred Prospero;
a Glenn Miller, Ray Noble;
VR Al Bowlley.

88963 **Paris in Spring** Vi 25040, HMV BD-192.
88964 **Bon Jour** Vi 25040, HMV BD-192.
88965 **Way Down Yonder in New Orleans** Vi 25082, HMV BD-263, HMV BD-5004, HMV 7EG 8056.
88966 **Chinatown, My Chinatown** Vi 25070, HMV MH-49.

27 May 1935 DORSEY BROTHERS' ORCHESTRA

TB Glenn Miller, Tommy Dorsey, Don Mattison;
TP George Throw;
S Jimmy Dorsey Clt & AS; Jack Stacy, Skeets Herfurt TS;
Rh Bob Van Epps P; Delmar Kaplan B; Roc Hillman G; Ray McKinley D;
VR Kay Weber, Bob Crosby.

39539 **Footloose and Fancy Free** De 182.
39540 **Every little Moment** De 480.
39541 **You're All I Need** De 182.
39542 **I'll Never Say "Never Again" Again** De 480.
39543 **Chasing Shadows** De 476.
39544 **Every Single Little Tingle of My Heart** De 476.

8 June 1935 RAY NOBLE and his ORCHESTRA

Same personnel as that of 10 May 1935.

92229 **Top Hat** Vi 25094, HMV BD-247.
92230 **Let's Swing It** Vi 25070, HMV MH-49.

10 June 1935 RAY NOBLE and his ORCHESTRA

Same personnel as that of 10 May 1935.

92231 **The Piccolino** Vi 25094, HMV BD-247.
92232 **St. Louis Blues** Vi 25082, HMV BD-263, HMV BD-5004.

20 July 1935 RAY NOBLE and his ORCHESTRA

Same personnel as that of 10 May 1935.

92747 **Why Dream?** Vi 25104, HMV BD-210.
92748 **Double Trouble** Vi 25105, HMV BD-211.
92749 **Why The Stars Come Out** Vi 25105, HMV BD-210.
92750 **I Wished on The Moon** Vi 25104, HMV BD-211.

1 August 1935 DORSEY BROTHERS' ORCHESTRA

Same personnel as that of 27 May 1935.

39797 **My Very Good Friend The Milkman** De 519.
39798 **You're So Gosh Darned Charming** De 520.
39799 **No Strings** De 516, BrE RL307.
39800 **Top Hat, White Tie, and Tails** De 516, BrE RL307.
39801 **You Saved My Life** De 520.
39802 **I Couldn't Believe My Eyes** De 519.

11 SEPTEMBER 1935 DORSEY BROTHERS' ORCHESTRA

Same personnel as that of 27 May 1935

39962	**The Gent obviously doesn't believe**	**De 561.**	
39963	**I've got a feeling you're fooling**	**De 560.**	
39964	**On a Sunday Afternoon**	**De 559.**	
39965	**You Are My Lucky Star**	**De 559.**	

18 SEPTEMBER 1935 RAY NOBLE and his ORCHESTRA

Same personnel as that of 10 May 1935, except—

AS Milt Yaner replaces "Toots" Mondello.

95042	**Roll Along Prairie Moon**	**Vi 25142.**	
95043	**Red Sails In The Sunset**	**Vi 25142.**	

9 OCTOBER 1935 RAY NOBLE and his ORCHESTRA

Same personnel as that of 18 September 1935.

95190	**Bugle Call Rag**	**Vi 25233,**	HMV BD-5197.
95191	**Dinah**	**Vi 25233,**	HMV BD-5197.

14 NOVEMBER 1935 RAY NOBLE and his ORCHESTRA

Same personnel as that of 18 September 1935.

98063	**Life Begins at Sweet Sixteen**	**Vi 25190.**	
98064	**I'm The Fellow Who Loves You**	**Vi 25190.**	
98065	**Where Am I**	**Vi 25187,**	HMV BD-5072.
98066	**Dinner For One**	**Vi 25187.**	

9 DECEMBER 1935 RAY NOBLE and his ORCHESTRA

Same personnel as that of 18 September 1935.

98359	**With All My Heart**	**Vi 25209,**	HMV BD-5028
98360	**I Built A Dream**	**Vi 25200.**	
98361	**Somebody Ought To Be Told**	**Vi 25200.**	
98362	**Beautiful Lady In Blue**	**Vi 25209.**	

23 JANUARY 1936 RAY NOBLE and his ORCHESTRA

TB Glenn Miller, Will Bradley;
TP Charlie Spivak, George "Pee Wee" Erwin;
S Johnny Mince Clt & AS; Milt Yaner AS; Jimmy Cannon BS; Bud Freeman, Dan D'Andrea TS;
Rh Claude Thornhill P; Delmar Kaplan B; George Van Epps G; Bill Harty D;
Vln Nick Pisani, Fred Prospero;
a Glenn Miller, Ray Noble;
VR Al Bowlley.

98670	**Let Yourself Go**	**Vi 25241,**	HMV BD-5047.
98671	**We Saw the Sea**	**Vi 25240,**	HMV BD-5046.
98672	**Let's Face The Music**	**Vi 25241,**	HMV BD-5047.
98673	**If You Love Me**	**Vi 25240,**	HMV BD-5046.

19 MARCH 1936 RAY NOBLE and his ORCHESTRA

Same personnel as that of 23 January 1936, except:

TP Sterling Bose (also VR) replaces "Pee Wee" Erwin.

99900	**Yours Truly, Truly Yours**	**Vi 25277.**	
99901	**Moonlight in Hilo**	**Vi 25282**	
99902	**The Touch Of Your Lips**	**Vi 25277.**	
99903	**Blazing The Trail**	**Vi 25282.**	

25 MAY 1936 RAY NOBLE and his ORCHESTRA

Same personnel as that of 19 March 1936.

101863	**Empty Saddles**	**Vi 25346,**	HMV BD-5095.
101864	**Big Chief De Sota**	**Vi 25346,**	HMV BD-5095.
101865	**But Definitely**	**Vi 25336.**	
101866	**When I'm With You.** VR, AB.	**Vi 25336.**	

15 SEPTEMBER 1936 BEN POLLACK and his ORCHESTRA

TB Glenn Miller, Bruce Squires;
TP Harry James, Shorty Sherock;
S Irving Fazola Clt; Opie Cates AS; Dave Matthews TS;
Rh Freddie Slack P; ThrumanTeague B; Frank Frederico G; Ben Pollack D
Vln Roy Cohen;
VR Lois Still.

19879	**I'm One Step Ahead of My Shadow**	**Br 7751,**	VoE 509.
19880	**Through the Courtesy of Love**	**Br 7747.**	
19881	**I Couldn't Be Mad At You**	**Br 7751.**	

Add Joe Price, Steel Guitar; Sammy Taylor D.

19882	**Song of the Islands**	**Br 7746,**	Co 36325.

16 SEPTEMBER 1936 BEN POLLACK and his ORCHESTRA

Same personnel as that of 15 September 1936, except Price & Taylor *out*.

19889	**Jim Town Blues**	**Br 7746,** Co 36325, VoE S-113.
19890	**Now or Never**	**Br 7747.**

OCTOBER 1936 CHUCK BULLOCK and his ORCHESTRA

TB Glenn Miller;
TP Harry James;
S Irving Fazola Clt & AS;
Rh Freddie Slack P; Ben Pollack D;
VR Chuck Bullock.

19991	**Let's Call a Heart a Heart**	**Me M-61212.**
19992	**You Do The Darndest Things**	**Me M-61212.**
19993	**I Can't Pretend**	**Me M-70103.**
19994	**When My Dreamboat Comes Home**	**Me M-70103,** Cq 8775.

17 JANUARY 1937—New York

MIFF MOLE and his ORCHESTRA

TB Glenn Miller, Miff Mole, Vincent Grande;
TP Harry James, Chris Griffin, Tony Tortommas;
S Paul Ricci Clt; Toots Mondello AS;
Rh Frank Signorelli P; Sid Weiss B; Carl Kress G; Sam Weiss D;
VR Midge Williams, Chuck Bullock.

20690	**On a Little Bamboo Bridge**	**Br 7842.**	
20691	**How Could You**	**Br 7842,**	VoE S-87.
20692	**I Can't Break The Habit of You**	**Vo 3468,**	VoE S-87.
20693	**Love and Learn**	**Vo 3468.**	

SECTION III

THE GLENN MILLER ORCHESTRAS, 1935—1942

25 APRIL 1935—Columbia recording session.

GLENN MILLER and his ORCHESTRA

Note : This was a studio recording group only; it is the same session as that on page 18, repeated here for convenience.

TB Glenn Miller, Jack Jenny;
TP Bunny Berigan, Charlie Spivak;
S Johnny Mince Clt & AS; Eddie Miller TS;
Rh Claude Thornhill P; Delmar Kaplan B; Larry Hall G; Ray Bauduc D;
St Harry Bluestone, Vladimir Selinski Vln; Bill Schumann 'Cello; Harry Waller Vla;
VR Smith Ballew.

17379 **A Blues Serenade.** VR, SB. **Co 3051-D,** Bi 1022.
17380 **Moonlight on the Ganges.** VR, SB. **Co 3051-D,** Bi 1022.
17381 **In a Little Spanish Town** **Co 3058-D,**
Bi 1045, Co 35881, CoE FB-1150.

Note:—Jack Jenny, TB, and the Strings *out.*

17382 **Solo Hop** (Pagan Love Song) **Co 3058-D,**
Bi 1045, Co 35881, CoE FB-1150, Epic EG 7005 (Epic issued under B. Berigan's name).

22 MARCH 1937—Decca recording session.

Note:—From here on the personnel of any session is the same as that of the preceding session, unless otherwise stated.

TB Glenn Miller, Jesse Ralph, Harry Rogers;
TP Charlie Spivak, Manny Klein, Sterling Bose;
S Hal McIntyre Clt & AS; George Siravo AS; Jerry Jerome, Carl Biesecker TS;
Rh Howard Smith P; Ted Kotsoftis B; Dick McDonough G; George Simon D.
VR Doris Kerr, Sterling Bose.

62058 **Peg O' My Heart** **De 1342,**
BrE 03807, De 25075, DeC 10113, DeF BM-03807, DeSp RB-45014.
62059 **Wistful and Blue.** VR, DK. **De 1284,** BrG 82574.
62060 **How am I to know** VR, DK. **De 1239,** BrE 02831.
62061 **Anytime, Anyday, Anywhere.**VR, SB. **De 1284.**
62062 **Moonlight Bay.** VR, Band. **De 1239,**
BrE 02402, BrE 03807, De 25075, DeF BM-03807, DeSp RB-45014.
62063 **I'm Sitting on Top of the World** **De 1342,** DeC 10113,
BrG 82574

9 JUNE 1937—New York, Brunswick recording session.

TS Johnny Harell replaces Carl Biesecker.

b 21234 **I Got Rhythm** **Br 7915,**
Bi 1046, Cq 9488, Epic LG-1008, Epic EG-7034, OK 5051, Vo 5051, CoE SCM 5086, CoE DB 3416. PhE BBR 8072.

b 21235 **Sleepy Time Gal** **Br 7923,**
Epic LG-1008, Epic EG-7034, OK 5051, CoE 3416, Poly 6002, Vo 5051, VoE 5127, CoE SCM 5086. PhE BBR 8072.

b 21236 **Community Swing** **Br 7923,**
Epic LG-1008, Epic EG-7012, Poly 6002. PhE BBR 8072.

b 21240 **Time On My Hands** **Br 7915,**
Bi 1046, Epic LG-1008, Epic EG-7034. PhE BBR 8072.

29 NOVEMBER 1937—New York, Brunswick recording session.

TB Glenn Miller, Jesse Ralph, Bud Smith;
TP George "Pee Wee" Erwin, Bob Price, Ardelle Garrett;
S Hal McIntyre, Tony Viola AS; Jerry Jerome, Carl Biesecker TS; Irving Fazola Clt;
Rh J. C. "Chummy" MacGregor P; Rowland Bundock B; Carmen Mastren G; Doc Carney D;
VR Kathleen Lane, Ray Eberle.

b 22079 **My Fine Feathered Friend.** VR, KL. **Br 8034.**

b 22080 **Humoresque** **Br 8062,**
Cq 9488, Epic LG-1008, Epic EG-7012, OK 4449, Poly 6001, Vo 4449, PhE BBR 8072.

b 22081 **Doin' The Jive.** VR, KL, Band. **Br 8062,**
Talking GM, JCMacGregor.
Cq 9489, Epic LG-1008, Epic EG-7012, OK 5131, Poly 6001, Vo 5131, PhE BBR 8072.

b 22082 **Silhouetted In Moonlight.** VR, KL. **Br 8034.**

13 DECEMBER 1937—Brunswick recording session.

b 22135 **Every Day's a Holiday.** VR, KL. **Br 8041,** Bi 1047.

b 22136 **Sweet Stranger.** VR, KL. **Br 8041,** Bi 1047.

FEBRUARY 1938

Glenn Miller disbands the orchestra, keeping five men with him to form the nucleus of a new orchestra (Bob Price TP; Hal McIntyre Clt & AS; J. C. "Chummy" MacGregor P; Rowland Bundock B; Ray Eberle VR).

23 MAY 1938—Brunswick recording session.

TB Glenn Miller, Al Mastren, Paul Tanner;
TP Bob Price, Johnny "Zulu" Austin, Gusparre Rebito;
S Hal McIntyre AS; Josh Billings AS & BS; Tex Beneke, Sol Kane TS; Wilbur Schwartz Clt;
Rh J. C. "Chummy" MacGregor P; Rowland Bundock B; Cody Sandifer D;
VR Solos: Gail Reese, Ray Eberle;
Quartet: Gail Reese, Ray Eberle, Sol Kane, Wilbur Schwartz.

b 22972 **Don't Wake Up My Heart.** VR, RE. **Br 8152,** Bi 1048.

b 22973 **Why'd Ya Make Me Fall in Love.** **Br 8152,** Bi 1048.
VR, GR.

b 22974 **Sold American** **Br 8173,**
Bi 1108, CoAu DO-2983, Epic LG-1008, Epic EG-7034, OK 5131, Vo 5131, PhE BBR 8072.

22975 **Dippermouth Blues** **Br 8173,**
Bi 1108, CoAu DO-2983, Cq 9489, Epic LG-1008, Epic EG-7012, OK 4449, Vo 4449, PhE BBR 8072.

Note:—On the sleeve of the Epic LP (LG 1008) the personnel for "Sold American" and "Dippermouth Blues" is wrongly given (by implication) as being the 1937 lineup. The same error occurs in "New Hot Discography" (1948) and is repeated on the English Philips LP.—*G.E.B.*

14 June 1938

Glenn Miller and his Orchestra open at the Paradise Restaurant in New York.

20 June 1938—Paradise Restaurant, New York, broadcast

Note:—Sixty selections were released by Victor in the "Glenn Miller Limited Edition, Vol. 2." They consisted entirely of broadcast recordings taken from this point until the Band disbanded in September 1942. In this listing it is referred to as "Vi GMLE 2." Other details on page 90.

E4VP 8208 (3: 09) **Doin' the Jive.** V, GR, TB, GM and Band. **Vi GMLE 2.**
E4VP 8208 (2: 45) **So Little Time** V, RE. **Vi GMLE 2.**

Note :—The personnels given in the Vi Album for these early broadcasts were entirely incorrect. Victor have supplied corrected information for much of the Album, not all of which, however, can be accepted unconditionally. For these four June broadcasts Victor give roughly the same personnel as on the 28 May recording session, *except* trumpets Johnny Austin, Bob Price and Gasparre Rebito; trombones Miller, Brad Jenny and Al Mastren; Stanley Aronson (sax) instead of Billings; Bob Spangler (dms) instead of Sandifer.—*G.E.B.*

25 June 1938—Paradise Restaurant, New York, broadcast.

E4 VP 8208 (3: 20) **Down South Camp Meeting** **Vi GMLE 2.**

27 June 1938—Paradise Restaurant, New York, broadcast.

E4VP 8208 (2: 54) **Humoresque** **Vi GMLE 2.**

July 1938

Glenn Miller and his Orchestra make their radio debut over the MBS Network

27 September 1938—Victor recording session.

TS Bill Stagmeir replaces Sol Kane.
027410 **My Reverie.** V, RE; a G. Miller (arrangement made for T. Dorsey) **BB 7853,** MW 7519, Poly 6005.
027411 **By the Waters of the Minnetonka,** Part 1. **BB 7870,** MW 7531, Poly 6004.
027412 **By the Waters of the Minnetonka,** Part 2. **BB 7870.** MW 7531, Poly 6004.
027413 **King Porter Stomp** **BB 7853,** HMVAu EA-2541, MW 7519, Poly 6005.
E2VL 4675 **By the Waters of the Minnetonka** (dubbed from 027411 & 027412) **Vi LPT-3036,** HMV DLP 1062, Vi 947-0091, Vi EPBT-3067, Vi LPT-3067.

23 December 1938—Paradise Restaurant, New York, broadcast

TB Glenn Miller, Al Mastren, Paul Tanner.
TP Johnny Austin, Bob Price, Leigh Knowles;
S (*probably*) Hal MacIntyre, Willie Schwartz, Tex Beneke, Bill Stagmeir, Stanley "Jim" Aronson.
Rh J. C. "Chummy" MacGregor P; Rowland Bundock B; Bob Spangler D.

E4VP 8208 (2: 22) **This Can't be Love.** VR, RE. **Vi GMLE 2.**

Note :—According to Victor (Jan. '55) a Jack Kimble (instrument unknown) played with the band some time during the period 23 December 1938 to 17 May 1939. This is uncorroborated.—*G.E.B.*

6 FEBRUARY 1939—Victor recording session.

TB Glenn Miller, Al Mastren, Paul Tanner;
TP Bob Price, Charlie Hill, Leigh Knowles;
S Hal MacIntyre, Willie Schwartz AS; Tex Beneke, Al Klink TS; Stanley Aronson AS & BS;
Rh J. C. "Chummy" MacGregor P; Roland Bundock B; Allan Reuss G; Cody Sandifer, D;
VR Marion Hutton, Ray Eberle, Tex Beneke.

Note :—In "Glenn Miller's Method for Orchestral Arranging" the doubling of instruments in the saxophone section is given as:

Bb Clar &	Eb Alto Sax	Schwartz
Eb Alto Sax	Bb Clar	Martin
Eb Alto Sax	Eb Bar. & Bb Clar.	Caceres.
Bb Tenor Sax	Bb Clar & Bb Bass Cl	Klink
Bb Tenor Sax	Bb Clar.	Beneke

It is not known whether this applied from the beginning of the band but if so, read MacIntyre for Martin and Aronson for Cacares.—*G.E.B.*

033607 **Gotta Get Some Shuteye.** VR, MH. **BB 10139,** RZ MR3028.
(Labelled "Wally Bishop & his Orch." on RZ)
033608 **How I'd Like To Be With You In Bermuda.** VR, RE. **BB 10139.**
033609 **Cuckoo In The Clock.** VR, MH. **BB 10145.**
033610 **Romance Runs in The Family** VR, MH. **BB 10145.**

4 APRIL 1939—Victor recording session

TP R. Dale McMickle replaces Charlie Hill;
D Frank Carlson replaces Cody Sandifer.

05399 **The Chestnut Tree.** VR, MH & Band **BB 10201,** MW 7965.
035700 **And the Angels Sing.** VR, RE. **BB 10201,** MW 7965.
035701-1/2/3 **Moonlight Serenade** **BB 10214.**
("Gone With The Wind")
GrF K-8644, HMV BD5942, HMV DLP1021, HMV DLP1024, HMVSw JK-2396, MW 7967, Polyd 10214, RZ MR3090, Vi 27-0028, Vi 42-0028, Vi 44-0007, Vi 947-0091, Vi 947-0136, Vi LPT-3036, Vi LPT-3057, Vi GMLE, ViJ 1020, V-D 39, Navy V-D 160.
035701-4 **Moonlight Serenade** (defective end) **Vi 20-1566.**
035702 **The Lady's in Love With You.** VR, TB, Talking GM & TB. **BB 10229.**
MW 7947, RZ MR3091.

4 APRIL 1939—Meadowbrook broadcast

E4VP 8205 (3:35) **Blue Skies** **Vi GMLE 2.**

Note:—According to Victor (Jan. '55) the drummer on this broadcast was either Spangler or Purtill. They do not mention Carlson.—*G.E.B.*

10 APRIL 1939—Victor recording session.

Note:—Seventy selections were released by Victor in the "Glenn Miller Limited Edition," including 29 BB and Vi studio recordings taken from this point until the Band disbanded in September 1942. In this listing it is referred to as "Vi GMLE." Other details on page 87. The Limited Edition has been issued in Europe by His Master's Voice.

D Maurice Purtill replaces Frank Carlson.

035729 **Wishing.** VR, RE. **BB 10219,**
HMV DLP 1049, Vi EPA 527, Vi GMLE, MW7968 RZ MR3117.

035730 **Three Little Fishes.** VR, MH & TB **BB 10219,** MW 7968.

035731 **Sunrise Serenade** **BB 10214,**
HMVAu EA-3318, HMV DLP 1062, MW 7967, Polyd 10214, RZ MR3090, Vi 20-1753, Vi 27-0028, Vi 42-0028, Vi 947-0090, Vi EPBT 3067, Vi EPA-527, Vi LPT-3036, Vi LPT-3067, ViJ1020.

035732 **Little Brown Jug.** a Bill Finegan. **BB 10286,**
HMV B10622, HMV 7M195, HMV DLP 1024, MW 7947, Vi 20-1566, Vi 47-2853, Vi EPA-148, Vi LPM-31.

18 APRIL 1939—Victor recording session.

G Arthur Enns replaces Alan Reuss.

035764 **My Last Goodbye.** VR, RE. **BB 10229,**
CoE DS1354, MW 7947.

035765 **But it didn't mean a thing.** VR, MH. **BB10269,** Vi 20-2972.

035766 **Pavanne** **BB 10286,**
HMV BD5805, HMV MH136, HMV DLP1081, Vi 20-2411, Vi 947-0039, Vi LPT-3002.

035767 **Running Wild** **BB 10269,**
HMV BD5805, HMV MH 136, HMV DLP 1062, Vi 20-2413, Vi 47-2877, Vi 947-0091, Vi EPBT-3067 Vi LPT-3036, Vi LPT-3067.

9 MAY 1939—Victor recording session.

AS & BS Gabriel Gelinas replaces Stanley "Jim" Aronson.

036877 **To You.** VR, RE. **BB 10276,**
HMVAu EA-2446, HMV 7EG8067, MW 8371, Vi LPT-1031, Vi EPAT-427.

036878 **Stairway to the Stars.** VR, RE. **BB 10276,**
HMV DLP 1049, MW 8371, RZ MR3117, Vi 20-3561.

17 MAY 1939

Glenn Miller and his Orchestra opens at the Glen Island Casino in New Rochelle, with broadcasts carried by both the NBC and MBS Networks.

TP By this time Clyde Hurley had replaced Bob Price.

E4VP 8203 (4:20) **At Sundown** **Vi GMLE 2**
E4VP 8204 (2:55) **And The Angels Sing** **Vi GMLE 2.**
VR, RE.

23 MAY 1939—Glen Island Casino broadcast.

E4VP 8205 (2: 22) **Get Out of Town.** **Vi GMLE 2.**
VR, RE.
E4VP 8206 (2: 48) **Deep Purple.** VR, RE. **Vi GMLE 2.**

Note:—In the GMLE 2 Album these broadcast items are incorrectly stated as coming from the Meadowbrook, as are those for May 26 and 31.
—*G.E.B.*

25 May 1939—Victor recording session.

037152 **Blue Evening.** VR, RE. **BB 10290,**
MW 8370, Vi 20-2889, Vi LPT-1016, Vi EPAT-429.
037153 **The Lamp Is Low.** VR, RE. **BB 10290,** MW 8370.
037154 **Rendezvous Time** In Paree. VR, RE **BB 10309.**
037155 **We Can Live On Love.** VR, MH. **BB 10309.**
037156 **Cinderella.** VR, RE. **BB 10303,** MW 8368.
037157 **Moon Love.** VR, RE. **BB 10303,**
HMV BD5854, HMV MH147, MW 8368.

26 May 1939—Glen Island Casino broadcast.

E4VP 8205 (2: 35) **Heaven Can Wait.** **Vi GMLE 2.**
VR, RE.
E4VP 8205 (1: 52) **We've Come a Long Way Together.**
VR, RE. **Vi GMLE 2.**

29 May 1939—Glen Island Casino broadcast.

E4VP 8203 (2: 48) **My Last Goodbye.** **Vi GMLE 2.**
VR, RE.
E4VP 8203 (3: 30) **Hallelujah** **Vi GMLE 2.**

31 May 1939—Glen Island Casino broadcast.

E4VP 8206 (2: 35) **My Heart Belongs to Daddy.**
VR, MH. **Vi GMLE 2.**

2 June 1939—Victor recording session.

AS & BS Harold Tennyson replaces Gabriel Gelinas;
G Richard Fisher replaces Arthur Enns.
037179 **I Guess I'll Go Back Home This Summer.** VR, TB. **BB 10317.**
037180 **I'm Sorry for Myself.** VR, TB. **BB 10299,**
Talking GM & TB.
(Labelled Vincent Lopez on RZ)
MW 8369, RZ MR3130.
037181 **Back to Back.** VR, MH. **BB 10299,** MW 8369.
037182 **Slip Horn Jive** **BB 10317,**
HMV BD5829, Vi GMLE.

13 June 1939—Glen Island Casino broadcast.

E4VP 8203 (5: 05) **The Hour of Parting** **Vi GMLE 2.**

20 June 1939—Glen Island Casino broadcast.

E4VP 8204 (2: 25) **We Can Live on Love.** **Vi GMLE 2.**
VR, MH.

22 June 1939—Victor recording session

TP John McGhee replaces Leigh Knowles.
037675 **Oh You Crazy Moon.** VR, RE. **BB 10329,** MW 8367.
037676 **Ain't You Comin' Out.** VR, MH, TB. **BB 10329** MW 8367.

27 June 1939—Victor recording session.

037699 **The Day We Meet Again.** VR, RE. **BB 10344,**
RZ MR3129, CoE DS-????
038200 **I wanna a hat with cherries.** VR, MH. **BB 10344.**
038201 **Sold American.** a GM. **BB 10352,**
GrF K-8644, HMV BD5854, HMV MH147, MW 8366.
038202 **Pagan Love Song** **BB 10352,**
HMV BD5839, HMVSp GY-620, MW 8366, ViJ 1165.

30 JUNE 1939—Glen Island Casino broadcast.

E4VP 8203 (2: 55) **I'm Sorry for Myself. Vi GMLE 2.**
VR, MH, TB & GM.

12 JULY 1939—Victor recording session.

038261 **Ding Dong the Witch is Dead.** V, MH. **BB 10366,**
HMV BD5546, HMVSp GY-455, MW 8364.

038262 **Over the Rainbow.** VR, RE. **BB 10366,**
HMV BD5546, HMVSp GY-455, MW 8364,
HMV 7EG8135.

038263 **The Little Man Who Wasn't There. BB 10358,** MW 8365,
VR, TB, Talking GM & TB.
HMV 7EG8097.

038264 **Man with the Mandolin.** VR, MH. **BB 10358,**
MW 8365, RZ MR 3129.

20 JULY 1939—Glen Island Casino broadcast.

E4VP 8203 (2: 30) **The Jumpin' Jive. Vi GMLE 2.**
VR, MH.

26 JULY 1939—Victor recording session.

VR Kay Starr replaces Marion Hutton.

038138 **Starlit Hour.** VR, RE. **BB 10553.**
HMV BD5929, HMV MH 145, Vi 20-3562.

038139 **Blue Orchids.** VR, RE. **BB 10372,**
HMV MH 104, MW 8363.

038140 **Glen Island Special.** a Will Hudson. **BB 10388,**
HMV BD5839, HMVSp GY-620, HMVSw JK-2232
MW 8361, Vi GMLE.

038141 **I'm in love with a Capital You. BB 10383,**
VR, KS. HMVSp GY-584, MW 8362, Vi GMLE.

038142 **Baby Me.** VR, KS. **BB 10372,**
MW 8363, Vi GMLE.

038143 **My Isle of Golden Dreams BB 10399,**
HMV BD5842, HMVSw JK-2309, MW 8360,
Vi 20-2412, Vi 947-0038, Vi LPT-3002,
HMV DLP1081,

26 JULY 1939—Glen Island Casino broadcast.

E4VP 8204 (2: 55) **Blue Orchids.** VR, RE. **Vi GMLE 2.**

28 JULY 1939—Glen Island Casino broadcast.

E4VP 8204 (3: 15) **Sunrise Serenade Vi GMLE 2.**

1 AUGUST 1939—Victor recording session.

VR Marion Hutton replaces Kay Starr.

038170 **In the Mood BB 10416,**
GrF K-8487, HMV BD5565, HMV DLP 1024,
HMVAu EA-2685, HMVSw JK-2047, MW 8358,
Vi 20-1565, Vi 20-1573, Vi 20-4086, Vi 47-2853,
Vi 47-4086, Vi 947-0136, Vi EPA-148, Vi LPM 31,
Vi LPT-3057, Vi EPA528, ViJ 1044, V-D 123.

038171 **Wham-Re-Bop-Boom-Bam.** VR, **BB 10399,**
MH, Band. HMVSw JK-2309, MW 8360, HMV MH181,
HMV 7EG8097.

038172 **An Angel in a Furnished Room.** VR, RE.
BB 10383, MW 8362.

038173 **Twilight Interlude.** VR, RE. **BB 10388,**
HMV MH158, HMVSw JK-2232, MW 8361.

038174 **I Want to be Happy** **BB 10416,**
HMV BD5585, MW 8358, ViJ 1044.

038175 **Farewell Blues** **BB 10495,**
HMV BD5602, HMV MH149, HMVSw JK-2326.

1 August 1939—Glen Island Casino broadcast.

E4VP 8204 (3: 01) **Twilight Interlude.** VR, RE. **Vi GMLE 2.**

15 August 1939—Glen Island Casino broadcast.

E4VP 8204 (3: 32) **Pagan Love Song** **Vi GMLE 2.**

18 August 1939—Victor recording session.

AS &BS Gerald Yelverton replaces Harold Tennyson.

041586 **Who's Sorry Now.** VR, RE. **BB 10486,**
HMV BD5697, HMV MH144.

041587 **My Prayer.** VR, RE. **BB 10404,**
HMV BD 5850, HMV MH142, HMVSw JK-2354,
ViJ 1158.

041588 **Blue Moonlight.** VR, RE. **BB 10404,**
HMV BD5822, HMV MH139, HMVSw JK-2422,
Vi J1158.

041589 **Basket Weaver Man.** VR, RE. **Vi 20-1585.**

23 August 1939.

Band closed at the Glen Island Casino after a record-breaking season; on this the final night there was an overflow crowd of 1200.

11 September 1939—Victor recording session.

TP John Best added;
TB Walter Barrow added.

042662 **Melancholy Lullaby.** VR, RE. **BB 10423,**
HMV BD5822, HMV MH139, HMVSw JK-2281,
MW 8645.

042663 **Why Couldn't It Last Last Night?** **BB 10423**
VR, RE. HMVSw JK-5822, MW 8645, RZ MR3198.

25 September 1939—Victor recording session.

TB Toby Tyler replaces Walter Barrow;
AS & BS Jimmy Abato replaces Gerald Yelverton.

042729 **Out of Space.** VR, RE. **BB 10438,**
GrF K-8487, HMV BD5565, HMVSw JK-2047.

042730 **So Many Times.** VR, RE. **BB 10438.**

2 October 1939—Victor recording session.

TB Tommy Mack replaces Toby Tyler.

042780 **Blue Rain.** VR, RE. **BB 10486,**
HMV BD5927, HMV 7EG8043, HMVSw JK-2412,
Vi EPAT-426, Vi 20-1536, Vi LPT 1031.

042781 **Can I Help It.** VR, RE. **BB 10448.**

042782 **I Just Got A Letter.** VR, MH. **BB 10448.**

6 OCTOBER 1939

The Glenn Miller Band took part in a special swing concert at Carnegie Hall, New York. They were the final band on the bill.

TB Glenn Miller, Al Mastren, Paul Tanner, Tommy Mack.
TP Clyde Hurley, Dale McMickle, John McGhee, John Best.
S Hal McIntyre AS, Willie Schwartz AS & Clt, Tex Beneke TS; Al Klink TS; Jimmy Abato AS & BS.
Rh J. C. "Chummy" MacGregor P; Roland Bundock B; Richard Fisher G; Maurice Purtill D.
VR Marion Hutton, Ray Eberle, Tex Beneke.

1. (1: 05) Introduction of Glenn Miller
2. (0:31) Moonlight Serenade
3. (2:39) Running Wild
4. (3:26) Sunrise Serenade
5. (2:55) Little Brown Jug
6. (1:46) Stairway to the Stars, VR, RE.
7. (1:40) To You. VR, RE.
8. (5:05) One O'Clock Jump
9. (1:55) Danny Boy.
10. (1:26) Jim Jam Jumpin' Jive. VR, MH.
11. (1:55) FDR Jones, VR, MH, Band.
12. (1:01) Hold Tight. VR, MH, Band.
13. (3:31) In the Mood.
14. (3:30) Bugle Call Rag.
15. (0:42) Moonlight Serenade

Note:—It was reported ("The Record Exchange," Toronto, December, 1951) that R.C.A. Victor declined to issue a recording of this Concert, and Columbia because Victor had better recordings of the tunes.—*G.E.B.*

9 OCTOBER 1939—Victor recording session.

042923 **Bless You.** VR, RE. **BB 10455,** MW 8644.
042924 **Bluebirds in the Moonlight.** VR, MH. **BB 10465,** HMVAu EA-2436, HMVSw JK-2281.
042925 **Faithful Forever.** VR, RE. **BB 10465,** HMV 7EG8135
042926 **Speaking of Heaven.** VR, RE. **BB 10455,** MW 8644.

5 NOVEMBER 1939—Victor recording session.

043354 **Indian Summer.** VR, RE. **BB 10495,** HMV BD5569, HMV DLP 1049, ViJ 1158.
043355 **It was written in the Stars.** VR, RE. **BB 10498,** HMV MH158, HMVAu EA-3345, HMVSw JK-2241.
043356 **Johnson Rag.** **BB 10498,** HMV BD5683, HMV MH140, HMVSw JK-2241, HMV DLP1081, Vi 20-2410, Vi 947-0038, Vi LPT-3002.

10 NOVEMBER 1939.

TB Frank D'Annolfo joined the band, replacing Tommy Mack who was actually the manager of the band.—*G.E.B.*

16 NOVEMBER 1939—Meadowbrook broadcast.

E4VP 8205 (3: 00) **I Want to be Happy** **Vi GMLE 2.**

18 NOVEMBER 1939—New York, Victor recording session.

TP Leigh Knowles replaces John McGhee.
043390 **Ciri-biri-bin.** VR, RE. **BB 10507,** HMV BD5842, MW 8641.
043391 **Careless.** VR, RE. **BB 10520,** HMV BD5569, Vi GMLE.
043392 **Oh Johnny, Oh Johnny.** VR, MH. **BB 10507,** MW 8641.

22 November 1939—New York, Victor recording session.

043909 **In an Old Dutch Garden.** VR RE. **BB 10553,**
HMVAu EA-2525.

043910 **This Changing World.** VR, RE. **BB 10526,**
HMVAu EA-3484.

043911 **On a little street in Singapore.** **BB 10526,**
VR, RE. Vi 20-1585, Vi GMLE.

043912 **Vagabond Dreams.** VR, RE. **BB 10520,**
HMV BD5585, HMV 7EG8043, Vi LPT-1031,
Vi EPAT-426.

24 November 1939—Meadowbrook broadcast.

E4VP 8206 (4: 52) **St. Louis Blues** **Vi GMLE 2.**
E4VP 8206 (3: 24) **Indian Summer.** VR, RE. **Vi GMLE 2.**

25 November 1939—Meadowbrook broadcast.

E4VP 8205 (2: 50) **Bluebirds in the Moonlight.** VR, MH.
Vi GMLE 2

26 November 1939—Meadowbrook broadcast.

E4VP 8206 (3: 50) **Tiger Rag** **Vi GMLE 2.**

6 December 1939—New York, Victor recording session.

043973 **I Beg Your Pardon.** VR, RE. **BB 10561.**
043974 **Faithful to You.** VR, RE. **BB 10536,**
HMV 7EG8067, HMVAu EA-2436, Vi **LPT-1031,**
Vi EPAT-427.

043975 **It's A Blue World.** VR, RE. **BB 10536,**
HMV BD 5587.

043976 **Oh What You Said.** VR, MH. **BB 10561.**

6 December 1939—Meadowbrook broadcast.

E4VP 8206 (2: 38) **After All.** VR, RE. **Vi GMLE 2.**

Note:—According to Victor (Nov. '53) John Wool (instrument unknown) played in the band from 7 to 14 December; also, Cliff Lash (instrument unknown) from 15 to 21 December. However, this is uncorroborated and nothing else is known of them.—*G.E.B.*

27 December 1939.

The Glenn Miller broadcasts sponsored by Chesterfield cigarettes begin over the CBS Network. For the first eleven weeks the Miller Band shared the programme with the Andrews Sisters, later taking over the whole programme themselves.

4 January 1940

Glenn Miller and his Orchestra open at the "Cafe Rouge" of the Hotel Pennsylvania, New York, broadcasting over the NBC Network

6 January 1940—New York, Victor recording session.

046082 **Gaucho Serenade.** VR, RE. **BB 10570,**
HMVAu EA-3556.

046083 **The Sky Fell Down.** VR, RE. **BB 10580.**
046084 **When You Wish Upon a Star.** VR, RE. **BB 10570,** Vi 20-3562,
HMV 7EG8135.

10 January 1940—Chesterfield Broadcast (Larry Bruff is Network announcer)

E3VP 5242 (4: 06) Medley:
My Melancholy Baby. Int GM.
Moon Love. VR, RE; Int GM.
Stompin' at the Savoy. Int, GM.
Blue Moon. Int. LB.
} **Vi GMLE**

15 January 1940—Victor recording session.

046431 **Give a little whistle.** VR, MH. **BB 10580,** HMV 7EG8135.
046432 **Missouri Waltz** **BB 10587,**
HMV BD-5644, HMVSw JK-2146, Vi 20-2411, Vi EPA-405, V-D 352, Vi LPT 1016.
046433 **Beautiful Ohio**—Waltz **BB 10587,**
HMV BD 5644, HMV DLP 1081, HMVSw JK-2146, Vi 947-0039, Vi LPT-3002.
046434 **What's the matter with me.** VR, MH. **BB 10657.**

24 January 1940—Chesterfield Broadcast

Al Mastren (tmb) out; Tommy Mack possibly replaced him.
E3VP 5237 (3: 20) Medley:
Japanese Sandman.
Int GM.
What's the matter with me.
VR, MH; Int GM.
Let's Dance. Int GM.
Blue Room. Int GM.
} **Vi GMLE**

26 January 1940—Victor recording session.

TB Tommy Mack definitely replaces Mastren.
046727 **Say Si Si.** VR, MH. **BB 10622,**
HMV BD-5602, HMV MH-149, Vi GMLE.
046728 **The Rhumba Jumps.** VR, MH, TB. **BB 10673,**
HMV 7EG8055, VdP GW-2023.

28 January 1940—Chesterfield Broadcast.

E3VP 5240 (4: 30) Medley:
Moon over Miami
Int GM.
A Million Dreams Ago.
VR, RE; Int GM.
Aloha. Int, GM.
} **Vi GMLE**
Blue Rain. Int, GM. (Bl. Rain not in GMLE)
(Timing of Bl. Rain not known).

29 January 1940—Victor recording session.

046735 **Star Dust** **BB 10665,**
HMV BD-5612, HMV MH-11, HMV DLP 1062, HMVSw JK-2279, Vi 20-1567, Vi 20-1754, Vi 47-2854, Vi EPA-405, Vi LPM-31, Vi LPT-3067, ViJ 1092.
046736 **My Melancholy Baby.** VR, TB. **BB 10665,**
HMV BD-5697, HMV MH-144, HMVSw JK-2279, Vi EPBT 3067, ViJ 1099, V-D 39.
046737 **Let's all sing together.** VR, MH. **BB 10598,** VdP GW-2077
046738 **Rug Cutter's Swing.** **BB 10754,**
HMV BD-5618, HMVAu EA-2780, HMVSw JK-2125, Vi GMLE.
046739 **Woodpecker Song.** VR, MH. **BB 10598,**
HMV BD-5587, HMV 7EG8055, HMVAu EA-2552, VdP GW-2077, Vi EPA 528.

4 February 1940—Chesterfield Broadcast.

V-4086 RR-17356 (2: 43) **Johnson Rag** **GMMS 4**, (*see also p.*91)
V-4086 RR-17356 (2: 13) **I'll never smile again.** **GMMS 4.**
VR, RE; Int, GM.
V-4086 RR-17356 (3: 10) **Wham-re-bop-boom-bam.** **GMMS 4.**
VR, MH, Band. Int, GM.
V-4086 RR-17356 (2: 25) **Fan Hat Stomp.** Int, GM. **GMMS 4.**
V-4086 RR-17356 (0: 18) **Moonlight Serenade.** **GMMS 4.**
Closing, GM.

5 February 1940—Victor recording session.

046784 **Sweet Potato Piper.** VR, MH, TB. **BB 10605,**
HMV BD-5596. HMV 7EG8055, HMVSw JK-2183.
046785 **Too Romantic.** VR, RE. **BB 10605,**
HMV BD-5596, HMVSw JK-2183.
046786 **Tuxedo Junction.** **BB 10612,**
HMV BD-5595, HMV DLP-1024, HMVAu EA-2541, HMVSw JK-2200, Vi 20-1552, Vi20-1565, Vi 20-1754, Vi 27-0085, Vi 947-0090, Vi 947-0137, Vi LPT-12, Vi LPT-3036, Vi LPT-3057, Vi EPA 528
046787 **Danny Boy.** Cls, GM. **BB 10612,**
HMV BD-5595, HMVSw JK-2200, HMV DLP 1081, Vi 947-0039, Vi LPT-3002.

19 February 1940—Victor recording session.

TB Jimmy Priddy, Replaces: Tommy Mack;
S Ernie Caceres, Replaces: Jim Abato AS; BS; Clt.
047067 **Imagination.** VR, RE. **BB 10622,**
HMV BD-5612, Vi GMLE.
047068 **Shake down the stars.** VR, RE. **BB 10689,** Vi 20-3562
047069 **I'll never smile again.** VR, RE. **BB 10673,**
HMV BD-1216, VdP GW-2023.
047070 **Starlight and Music.** VR, RE. **BB 10684,**
HMVAu EA-3337.

24 February 1940—Victor recording session.

047093 **Polka dots and moonbeams.** VR, RE. **BB 10657.**
047094 **My My.** VR, MH. **BB 10631,** HMV BD-5606.
047095 **Say It.** VR, RE. **BB 10631,** HMV BD-5606.
047096 **Moments in the Moonlight.** VR, RE. **BB 10638.**
047097 **Hear My Song Violetta.** VR, RE. **BB 10684,**
HMV BD-5664, HMV DLP 1049, HMV 7EG8055.
047098 **Sierra Sue.** VR, RE. **BB 10638,**
HMV BD-5626, HMVAu EA-2625.

7 March 1940—Chesterfield Broadcast

V-4086 WR-936 (2: 40) **Guess I'll have to change my plans.** VR, MH, TB. **GMMS 2.**
V-4086 WR-936 (5: 25) Medley: **GMMS 2.**
My Darling. Int, GM.
Blueberry Hill. VR, RE; Int., GM.
I can't get started. Int, GM.
Blue. Int, GM.
V-4086 WR-936 (2: 45) **My Blue Heaven.** Int, GM **GMMS 2.**

10 MARCH 1940—Chesterfield Broadcast.

E3VP 5244 (2: 20) **Bless You.** VR, RE. **Vi GMLE.**

12 MARCH 1940—Chesterfield Broadcast.

E3VP 5241 (2: 35) **King Porter Stomp.** **Vi GMLE.**

19 MARCH 1940—Chesterfield Broadcast.

V-4086 WR-963 (2: 38) **Stardust.** **GMMS 15,** GMMS 63.
V-4086 WR-963 (4: 16) Medley: **GMMS 15,** GMMS 63.
Can't you hear me calling Caroline. Int, GM.
Sweet Potato Piper, Int, GM; VR, MH, TB.
V-4086 WR-963 (3: 04) **Pagan Love Song.** Int GM. **GMMS 15,** GMMS 63.
E2VL 4545 (2: 10) **Dippermouth Blues,** a GM. **Vi LPT-3001,** HMV DLP-1021, Vi 947-0054
E4VP 8210 (2: 25) **I'll never smile again.** VR, RE. **Vi GMLE 2.**
E4VP 8210 (2: 30) **Sophisticated Lady** **Vi GMLE 2.**

Note:—According to Victor (Jan. '55), some time during the period 6 December 1939 to May 10 1940 Charlie Hill (TP) and Cody Sandifer (D) played with the band. This is contrary to all other published information (although both men certainly played with the band a year earlier) and seems rather suspect.—*G.E.B.*

22 MARCH 1940—Chesterfield broadcast.

E4VP 8207 (1: 25) **Be Happy.** VR, MH. **Vi GMLE 2.**
E4VP 8207 (3: 45) **Georgia on my mind** **Vi GMLE 2.**

26 MARCH 1940—Chesterfield broadcast.

V-4086 RR-17357 (3: 55) **Pennsylvania 6-5000.** VR, Band. **GMMS 3.**
V-4086 RR-17357 (2: 05) **Let's all sing together.** VR, MH; Int. GM. **GMMS 3.**
V-4086 RR-17357 (2: 39) **Moonlight Serenade.** Int, GM. **GMMS 3.**
V-4086 RR-17357 (2: 51) **Slip Horn Jive.** Int, GM. **GMMS 3.**

30 MARCH 1940—Victor recording session.

048482 **Boog It.** VR, MH, Band. **BB 10689,** HMV BD-5626.
048483 **Yours is my heart alone.** **BB 10728,**
(H.M.V. labelled as "You are my Heart's Delight".)
HMV BD-5664, HMV DLP 1049.
048484 **I'm stepping out with a memory, Tonight.** VR, RE. **BB 10717,**
HMV BD-5617, VdP GW-2000.
048485 **Alice Blue Gown**—Waltz. **BB 10701,**
HMV BD-5654, HMV DLP 1049, HMVSw JK-2169, Vi EPA-405, Vi LPT 1016, V-D 352.
048486 **Wonderful One**—Waltz. **BB 10701,**
HMV BD-5654, HMVSw JK-2169, Vi GMLE.
048487 **Devil May Care.** VR, RE. **BB 10717,**
HMV BD-5617, Vi GMLE.

31 March 1940—Victor recording session.

048488 **April played the fiddle.** VR, RE. **BB 10694,**
HMV 7EG 8043, Vi LPT 1031, Vi EPAT-426.
048489 **Fools Rush In.** VR, RE. **BB 10728.** Vi GMLE.
048490 **I haven't time to be a millionaire.** **BB 10694.**
VR, TB.
048491 **Slow Freight.** **BB 10740,** HMV BD-5633.

March 1940—Chesterfield Broadcast. The exact date of broadcast in March is unknown.

V-4086 WR-1108 (3: 35) **Stardust.** **GMMS 45.**
V-4086 WR-1108 (4: 07) Medley: **GMMS 45**
Hat with Cherries.
VR, MH. Int GM.
Story of a starry night.
VR, RE; Int, GM.
V-4086 WR-1108 (4: 13) **Tuxedo Junction.** Int, GM. **GMMS 45.**

1 April 1940—Chesterfield Broadcast.

V-4086 WR-956 (2: 38) **On the Alamo** **GMMS 9,** GMMS 57.
V-4086 WR-956 (5: 05) Medley: **GMMS 9,** GMMS 57.
Cabana in Havana. VR, MH.
I'll never smile again.
VR, RE; Int, GM.
V-4086 WR-956 (3: 45) **St. Louis Blues.** **GMMS 9,** GMMS 57.
Int, GM, LB.
V-4086 WR-956 (0: 30) **Moonlight Serenade** **GMMS 9,** GMMS 57

4 April 1940—Broadcast.

E3VP 5243 (3: 48) **One O'Clock Jump.** **Vi GMLE.**

8 April 1940.

Glenn Miller and his Orchestra draws 6500 in the Baltimore Coliseum.

9 April 1940—Chesterfield Broadcast.

V-4086 WR-987 (2: 58) **Slow Freight.** **GMMS 27,** GMMS 75.
V-4086 WR-987 (3: 45) Medley: **GMMS 27,** GMMS 75.
Fools Rush In. Int, GM.
Woodpecker Song. VR, MH; Int, GM.
V-4086 WR-987 (3: 41) **King Porter Stomp.** **GMMS 27,** GMMS 75.

10 April 1940—Chesterfield Broadcast.

WR-952 (1: 50) **Outside of that I love you.** **GMMS 5,** GMMS 53.
VR, MH, TB.
WR-952 (3: 00) **The Gentleman needs a Shave.** VR, MH, TB. **GMMS 5,** GMMS 53.
WR-952 (2: 50) **When the swallows come back to Capistrano.** **GMMS 5,** GMMS 53.
VR, RE; Int, GM.
WR-952 (3: 00) **Everybody loves my baby.** **GMMS 5,** GMMS 53.
Int, GM, LB.

18 APRIL 1940—Chesterfield Broadcast.

V-4086 WR-983 (2: 08) **Anchors Aweigh** **GMMS 23,** GMMS 71
V-4086 WR-983 (1: 55) **Fools Rush In** **GMMS 23,** GMMS 71
V-4086 WR-983 (3: 00) **The Weekend of a Private Secretary**
VR, MH; Int. GM. **GMMS 23,** GMMS 71
Vi GMLE. (No Miller Int on GMLE)
V-4086 WR-983 (4: 22) **Tuxedo Junction** **GMMS 23,** GMMS 71

23 APRIL 1940—Chesterfield Broadcast

E2VL 4419 (1: 58) **I Dream of Jeannie with the Light Brown Hair** **Vi LPT-30**
HMV MH-172, HMV DLP 1012, Vi 27-0155
Vi 42-0155 Vi 947-0026.

25 APRIL 1940—Chesterfield Broadcast.

WR-979 (2: 48) **On The Alamo** **GMMS 19,** GMMS 67
WR-979 (5: 10) Medley: **GMMS 19,** GMMS 67
Let's All Sing Together.
VR, MH; Int GM.
Say It. VR, RE; Int GM.
WR-979 (2:44) **Fan Hat Stomp.** a Eddie Barefield.
E2VL 4545 Int GM, LB. **GMMS 19,**
GMMS 67, HMV DLP-1013, Vi 947-0055,
Vi LPT-3001.

28 APRIL 1940—Victor recording session.

TP Reuben "Zeke" Zarchey, replaces: R. Dale McMickle;
G Jack Lathrop G, VR, replaces: Richard Fisher.

048963 **Pennsylvania 6-5000.** VR, Band. **BB 10754,**
HMV BD-5618, HMV DLP-1024, HMVSw JK-2125, VdP GW-2000, Vi 20-1567, Vi 47-2877 Vi 947-0136, Vi EPA-405, Vi LPM-31, Vi LPT-3057
048964 **Bugle Call Rag.** **BB 10740,**
HMV BD-5633, HMV DLP1062, Vi 20-2413, Vi 47-2877, Vi 947-0090, Vi LPT-3036, Vi EPBT 3067, Vi LPT 3067.
048965 **The Nearness of You.** VR, RE. **BB 10745,**
HMV BD-5632, HMV MH-92, HMV 7EG8067, HMVAu EA-2736, Vi LPT1031, Vi EPAT-427.
048966 **W.P.A.** VR, TB, Band. BB Unissued.
048967 **Mister Meadowlark.** VR, JL. **BB 10745,** Vi GMLE.
048968 **My Blue Heaven** **BB 10994,**
HMV BD-5678, HMVSw JK-2323, ViJ 1092.

APRIL 1940—Chesterfield Broadcasts.

Note:—The following broadcasts were aired in April 1940, but the exact broadcast date in April is unknown.

V-4086 WR-953 (2:30) **T'ain't no use at all** **GMMS 6,** GMMS 54.
V-4086 WR-953 (5:30) Medley: **GMMS 6,** GMMS 54.
Goodnight Sweetheart. Int, GM.
I'm stepping out with a memory tonight. VR, RE; Int, GM.
When my baby smiles at me. Int, LB.
Blues Serenade. Int, GM.

V-4086 WR-953 (2: 40) **Runnin' Wild.** Int, GM. GMMS 6, GMMS 54.
V-4086 WR-954 (2: 27) **Runnin' Wild.** GMMS 7, GMMS 55.
V-4086 WR-954 (2: 01) **Polka dots and moonbeams.** Int, GM. GMMS 7, GMMS 55.
V-4086 WR-954 (2: 06) **FDR Jones.** VR, MH; Int, GM. GMMS 7, GMMS 55.
V-4086 WR-954 (1: 45) **Drink to me only with thine eyes.** Int, LB. GMMS 7, GMMS 55.
V-4086 WR-955 (3: 15) **Wham-re-bop-boom-bam.** VR, MH, Band. GMMS 8, GMMS 56.
V-4086 WR-955 (4: 40) Medley: GMMS 8, GMMS 56.
Peg O' My Heart. Int, GM.
Polka Dots and Moonbeams.
VR RE; Int, GM.
Mood Indigo. Int, LB.
Blue Orchids. Int, LB.
V-4086 WR-955 (3: 20) **Down for the count** Int, GM. GMMS 8, GMMS 56.
V-4086 WR-962 (3: 16) **Sunrise Serenade** GMMS 14, GMMS 62.
V-4086 WR-962 (4: 52) Medley: GMMS 14, GMMS 62.
The gentleman needs a shave.
VR, MH, TB; Int, GM.
The story of a starry night.
VR, RE; Int, GM.
V4086 WR-962 (2: 38) **In the Mood.** Int, GM. GMMS14, GMMS62.
V-4086 WR-965 (2: 33) **Rug Cutter's Swing.** GMMS 17, GMMS 65.
V-4086 WR-965 (5: 14) Medley: GMMS 17, GMMS 65.
Outside of that, I love you.
VR, MH, TB.
String of Pearls.
V-4086 WR-965 (3: 16) **Slip Horn Jive.** GMMS 17, GMMS 65.
V-4086 WR-1114 (2: 56) **Sunrise Serenade.** GMMS 42.
V-4086 WR-1114 (4: 57) Medley: GMMS 42.
Let's all sing together.
VR, MH; Int, GM.
April played the fiddle.
VR RE; Int, GM.
V-4086 WR-1114 (2: 39) **Fan Hat Stomp.** Int LB, GM. GMMS 42.

2 May 1940—Chesterfield Broadcast.

TB Glenn Miller, Paul Tanner, Frank D'Annolfo, Jimmy Priddy;
TP Leigh Knowles, Zeke Zarchey, Clyde Hurley, John Best;
S Hal McIntyre, Wilbur Schwartz AS; Tex Beneke, Al "Mose" Klink TS; Ernie Caceres AS and BS;
Rh J. C. "Chummy" MacGregor P; Rowland Bundock B; Jack Lathrop G; Maurice Purtill D.
VR Marion Hutton, Ray Eberle, Tex Beneke, Jack Lathrop.

V-4086 WR-1030 (2: 12) **I want to be happy.** GMMS 28, GMMS 76.
V-4086 WR-1030 (4: 18) Medley: GMMS 28, GMMS 76.
Cowboy from Brooklyn.
VR, MH, TB; Int, LB.
Sierra Sue. VR, RE; Int, GM.
V-4086 WR-1030 (4: 03) **In the Mood.** Int, GM. GMMS 28, GMMS 76.

8 May 1940—Chesterfield Broadcast.

E1LVB 3200 (3: 44) **One O'Clock Jump.** **Vi LPT-16,**
Int, GM.
HMV DLP-1021, Vi 27-0107, Vi 42-0107
Vi 947-0024.

10 May 1940—Chesterfield Broadcast.

E4VP 8209 (2: 45) **Body and Soul.** **Vi GMLE 2.**
E4VP 8209 (2: 47) **The Rhumba Jumps.** **Vi GMLE 2.**
VR, MH & TB.

15 May 1940—Chesterfield Broadcast.

E1LVB 3200 (3: 42) **St. Louis Blues.** Int GM. **Vi LPT-16,**
HMV DLP-1021, Vi 27-0109, Vi 42-0109,
Vi 947-0024.

16 May 1940—Chesterfield Broadcast.

V-4086 WR-1029 (3: 57) **One O'Clock Jump.** **GMMS 40.**
V-4086 WR-1029 (5: 34) Medley: **GMMS 40**
When you wish upon a Star. VR, RE; Int, GM.
Cabana in Havana. VR, MH.
V-4086 WR-1029 (2: 38) **Caribbean Clipper** **GMMS 40.**

22 May 1940—Chesterfield Broadcast.

V-4086 WR-982 (1: 53) **Woodpecker song.** VR, MH. **GMMS 22,** GMMS 70.
V-4086 WR-982 (5: 56) Medley: **GMMS 22,** GMMS 70.
Poor Butterfly. Int, GM.
The sky fell down. VR, RE; Int, GM.
I'm getting sentimental over you. Int, LB.
Black and Blue. Int, LB.
V-4086 WR-982 (4: 04) **By the waters of the Minnetonka.** Int GM, LB. **GMMS 22,** GMMS 70.

May 1940—Chesterfield Broadcasts. The exact date of broadcast in May is unknown.

V-4086 WR-964 (2: 38) **Say Si Si.** VR, MH. **GMMS 16,** GMMS 64
V-4086 WR-964 (5: 38) Medley: **GMMS 16,** GMMS 64
Goodnight Sweetheart, Int, GM.
I'm stepping out with a memory tonight. VR, RE; Int, GM.
When my baby smiles at me. Int, LB.
A Blues Serenade. Int, GM.
V-4086 WR-964 (3: 12) **Bugle Call Rag.** Int, GM. **GMMS 16,** GMMS 64.
V-4086 WR-966 (3: 08) **Conversation Piece.** **GMMS 18,** GMMS 66.
V-4086 WR-966 (3: 51) Medley: **GMMS 18,** GMMS 66.
I wanna hat with cherries. VR, MH; Int, GM.
Polka Dots and Moonbeams. VR, RE; Int, GM.
V-4086 WR-966 (4: 23) **St. Louis Blues.** Int. GM. **GMMS 18.** GMMS 66.

2 June 1940—Chesterfield Broadcast.

TP Charles Frankhauser replaces Clyde Hurley;
TP R. Dale McMickle replaces Leigh Knowles.

E3VP 5238 (2: 57) **Little Brown Jug.** **Vi GMLE**
Vi 947-0137, Vi LPT-3057.

4 June 1940—Chesterfield Broadcast.

E3VP 5243 (2: 20) **Oh Lady be Good.** **Vi GMLE.**
E1LVB 3201 (3: 22) **My Blue Heaven.** **Vi LPT-16,**
HMV DLP-1013, Vi 27-0107, Vi 42-1007, Vi 947-0025.
E1LVB 3201 (0: 03) **Moonlight Serenade.** **Vi LPT-16,**
HMV DLP-1013, Vi 27-0107, Vi 42-1007, Vi 947-0025.

13 June 1940—Chicago, Victor recording session

053130 **When the swallows come back to Capistrano.** VR, RE. **BB 10776,** HMV MH-99
053131 **A Million Dreams Ago.** VR, RE. **BB 10768,**
HMV BD-5929, HMV MH-145, VdP GW-1984.
053132 **Blueberry Hill.** VR, RE. **BB 10768,**
HMV BD-5632, HMV MH-92, HMVAu EA-2723.
053133 **A Cabana in Havana.** VR, MH. **BB 10776,**
HMV MH-104, HMVAu EA-3351.
053134 **Be Happy.** VR, RE. **BB 10796,** VdP GW-1984.
053135 **Angel Child.** VR, RE. **BB 10796,** Vi GMLE.

June 1940—Chesterfield Broadcasts. The exact date of broadcast in June is unknown.

V-4086 WR-958 (5: 04) Medley: **GMMS 10,** GMMS 58.
My Isle of Golden Dreams.
Devil May Care. VR, RE; Int GM.
V-4086 WR-958 (2: 02) **Let's all sing together.** **GMMS 10,** GMMS 58.
VR, MH, Studio Audience;
Int, GM.
V-4086 WR-958 (3: 37) **Everybody loves my baby** **GMMS 10,** GMMS 58.
Int, GM, LB.
V-4086 WR-959 (2: 27) **Oh Lady be Good** **GMMS 11,** GMMS 59.
V-4086 WR-959 (4: 33) Medley: **GMMS 11,** GMMS 59.
I'll never smile again.
.VR, RE; Int, GM.
Say Si Si. VR, MH; Int, GM.
V-4086 WR-959 (3: 44) **My Blue Heaven.** Int, GM. **GMMS 11,** GMMS 59.

10 July 1940—Chesterfield Broadcast.

V-4086 WR-960 (3: 48) **One O'Clock Jump.** **GMMS 12,** GMMS 60.
V-4086 WR-960 (4: 14) Medley: **GMMS 12,** GMMS 60.
When you wish upon a star.
VR, RE; Int, GM.
Be Happy. VR, MH; Int, GM.
V-4086 WR-960/1104 (3: 35) **On brave old Army Teams.** **GMMS 12,** GMMS 48.
Int, GM.
"A Salute to the Boys at West Point." GMMS 60.

Note:—Victor reported (Nov. '53) that an E. Kenyon (instrument unknown) played with the band from 6 July to 25 October; however, this is uncorroborated and as nothing else is known of Kenyon we have omitted him entirely.—*G.E.B.*

11 July 1940—Chesterfield Broadcast.

E2VL 4420 (2: 36) **On the Alamo.** **Vi LPT-30,** HMV DLP-1012, Vi 27-0153, Vi 42-0153, Vi 947-0027.

19 July 1940—Chesterfield Broadcast.

V-4086 WR-961 (2: 10) **Jeannie with the light brown hair.** **GMMS 13,** GMMS 61.
V-4086 WR-961 (5: 27) Medley: **GMMS 13,** GMMS 61.
Outside of that I love you.
VR, MH, TB; Int, GM.
Handful of Stars.
VR, RE; Int, GM.
V-4086 WR-961 (3: 42) **King Porter Stomp.** **GMMS 13,** GMMS 61.
Int, GM, LB.

24 July 1940—Chesterfield Broadcast.

E3VP 5237 (3: 05) **Down for the Count.** **Vi GMLE.**

31 July 1940—Chesterfield Broadcast.

E3VP 5239 (2: 30) **I guess I'll have to change my plans.** VR, MH, TB. **Vi GMLE.**
E3VP 5239 (3: 51) Medley:
My Darling. Int, GM.
Blueberry Hill.
VR, RE; Int, GM.
I can't get started.
Int, GM.
} **Vi GMLE.**
(1: 44) **Blue.** Int, GM.
("Blue" is not included in Vi GMLE).

July 1940—Chesterfield Broadcasts. The exact date of broadcast in July is unknown.

V-4086 WR-1104 (3: 32) **On the Alamo.** **GMMS 48.**
V-4086 WR-1104 (4: 40) Medley: **GMMS 48.**
Can't you hear me calling, Caroline. Int, GM.
Handful of Stars.
VR, RE; Int, GM.
V-4086 WR-1106 (2: 40) **Whatcha know Joe?** **GMMS 50.**
VR, TB, Band.
V-4086 WR-1106 (4: 50) Medley: **GMMS 50.**
Fools Rush In.
VR, RE; Int, GM.
Weekend of a Private Secretary. VR, MH; Int, GM.
V-4086 WR-1106 (3: 35) **Oh So Good.** VR, Band. **GMMS 50.**

VR Paula Kelly replaces Marion Hutton.

V-4086 WR-1107 (3: 00) **Slow Freight.** **GMMS 52.**
V-4086 WR-1107 (4: 52) Medley: **GMMS 52.**
Little bit south of North Carolina. VR, PK; Int, GM.
High on a Windy Hill.
VR, RE; Int, GM.

V-4086 WR-1107 (3: 05) **Pagan Love Song.** Int GM GMMS 52.

VR Marion Hutton replaces Paula Kelly.

V-4086 WR-1110 (2: 10) **Jeannie with the light brown hair.** **GMMS 47.**

V-4086 WR-1110 (6: 00) Medley: **GMMS 47.**
Peg O' My Heart. Int, GM.
Polka Dots and Moonbeams. VR, RE; Int, GM.
Mood Indigo. Int, LB.
Blue Orchids. Int, LB.

V-4086 WR-1110 (3: 50) **St. Louis Blues.** Int, LB, GM. **GMMS 47.**

6 August 1940—Chesterfield Broadcast.

WR-1006 (2: 30) **I'll take you home again, Kathleen.** **GMMS 26, GMMS 77.**

WR-1006 (5: 08) Medley: **GMMS 26, GMMS 77.**
I haven't time to be a Millionaire. VR, MH, TB; Int GM.
I'll never smile again. VR, RE; Int GM.

WR-1006 (3: 30) **Down for the Count.** **GMMS 26, GMMS 77.**

8 August 1940—New York—Victor recording session.

055501 **Call of the Canyon.** VR, RE. **BB 10845.**
055502 **Our Love Affair.** VR, RE. **BB 10845,** HMVSp GY584.
055503 **Cross Town.** VR, JL. **BB 10832,** HMVAu EA-2685.
055504 **What's your story, mornin' glory.** VR, TB. **BB 10832,** HMVAu EA-2685.

8 August 1940—Chesterfield Broadcast.

V-4086 WR-1008 (1: 49) **My My.** VR, MH. **GMMS 31, GMMS 79.**

V-4086 WR-1008 (5: 33) Medley: **GMMS 31, GMMS 79.**
My Darling, Int GM.
Blueberry Hill. VR, RE; Int GM.
I can't get started. Int GM.
Blue. Int GM.

V-4086 WR-1008 (4: 15) **Tuxedo Junction.** Int GM. **GMMS 31,** GMMS 79

14 August 1940—New York—Victor recording session.

055515 **Fifth Avenue.** VR, MH. **BB 10860,** HMVAu EA-2634.
055516 **I wouldn't take a million.** VR, RE. **BB 10860**
055517 **Handful of Stars.** VR, RE. **BB 10893,** HMV MH 181, HMVSw JK-2134, Vi 20-3563
055518 **Old Black Joe.** **BB 10913,** HMV 7EG 8077, ViJ 1101.

14 August 1940—Chesterfield Broadcast.

V-4086 WR-1007 (3: 20) **Solitude.** **GMMS 30,** GMMS 78.
V-4086 WR-1007 (4: 22) Medley: **GMMS 30,** GMMS 78.
Be Happy. VR, MH; Int, GM.
I'm stepping out with a memory tonight. VR, RE.
V-4086 WR-1007 (4: 08) **My Blue Heaven.** Int GM. **GMMS 30,** GMMS 78.

15 August 1940—Chesterfield Broadcast.

V-4086 WR-1028 (3: 35) **My Buddy** **GMMS 39.**
V-4086 WR-1028 (4: 25) Medley: **GMMS 39.**
Polka Dots and Moonbeams VR, RE; Int GM.
FDR Jones. VR, MH, Band; Int GM.
V-4086 WR-1028 (4: 06) **Volga Boatmen.** **GMMS 39.**

22 August 1940—Chesterfield Broadcast

V-4086 WR-1009 (3: 07) **What's your story, mornin' Glory.** **GMMS 32,** GMMS 80.
V-4086 WR-1009 (5: 27) Medley: **GMMS 32,** GMMS 80.
I wanna hat with cherries. VR, MH; Int GM.
Fools Rush In. VR, RE; Int GM.
V-4086 WR-1009 (3: 10) **Solid as a stone wall, Jackson.** Int GM. **GMMS 32,** GMMS 80.

27 August 1940—Chesterfield Broadcast.

V-4086 WR-980 (2: 02) **Jeannie with the light brown hair.** **GMMS 20,** GMMS 68.
V-4086 WR-980 (5: 51) Medley: **GMMS 20,** GMMS 68.
I never took a lesson in my life. VR, MH, TB; Int GM.
When the swallows come back to Capistrano. VR, RE; Int GM.
V-4086 WR-980 (3: 26) **I want to be happy.** **GMMS 20,** GMMS 68.
V-4086 WR-980 (2: 37) **My Buddy.** **GMMS 24,** GMMS 68.
V-4086 WR-980 (6:00) Medley: **GMMS 24,** GMMS 68.
Wham-re-bop-boom-bam. VR, MH, Band; Int GM.
High on a windy hill. VR, RE; Int GM.
V-4086 WR-980 (2: 32) **Caribbean Clipper.** **GMMS 24,** GMMS 68.

28 August 1940—Chesterfield Broadcast.

V-4086 WR-1010 (3: 15) **Little Brown Jug** **GMMS 33,** GMMS 81.
V-4086 WR-1010 (5: 05) Medley: **GMMS 33,** GMMS 81.
I wouldn't take a million. VR, RE; Int GM.
A Tisket a Tasket. VR, MH; Int GM.
V-4086 WR-1010 (3: 36) (**Farewell Blues.** Int LB. **GMMS 33,**
E3VP 5245 (**Moonlight Serenade.** Closing announcement by GM GMMS 81, Vi GMLE.

28 AUGUST 1940

Glenn Miller and his Orchestra draw 1100 at the Municipal Auditorium in Kansas City.

29 AUGUST 1940—Chesterfield Broadcast.

V-4086 WR-1011 (1: 53) **Window shopping on Fifth Avenue.** **GMMS 34,** GMMS 82.
V-4086 WR-1011 (6: 20) Medley: **GMMS 34,** GMMS 82.
In the Mood. Int GM, LB.
Nearness of You.
VR, RE; Int GM.
V-4086 WR-1011 (4: 16) **Runnin' Wild.** Int GM. **GMMS 34,** GMMS 82.

AUGUST 1940—Chesterfield Broadcast. The exact date of broadcast in August is unknown.

V-4086 WR-1103 (3: 10) **Solitude.** **GMMS 49.**
V-4086 WR-1103 (5: 05) Medley: **GMMS 49.**
My My. VR, MH; Int GM.
You Walked By. VR, RE; Int GM.
V-4086 WR-1103 (4: 02) **Song of the Volga Boatmen.** **GMMS 49.**

3 SEPTEMBER 1940—Victor recording session.

B Tony Carlson, replaces: Rowland Bundock.
055579 **Yesterthoughts.** VR, RE. **BB 10893,** HMVSw JK-2134.
055580 **Falling Leaves.** **BB 10876,** HMV BD-5651, HMVAu EA-3318.
055581 **Shadows on the Sand.** VR, RE. **BB 10900,** HMV MH-95.
055582 **Goodbye, Little Darling, Goodbye.** VR, RE. **BB 10931,** HMVAu EA-3351, HMVSw JK-2252.

10 SEPTEMBER 1940

Glenn Miller and his Orchestra draws 3500 at the Buckley Lake Dancetaria, Ohio.

12 SEPTEMBER 1940—Victor recording session.

056106 **Five O'Clock Whistle.** VR, MH. **BB 10900.**
056107 **Beat me Daddy, Eight to the Bar.** VR, JL. **BB 10876,** HMV BD-5651
056108 **Ring Telephone Ring.** VR, RE. **BB 11042.**

12 SEPTEMBER 1940—Chesterfield Broadcast.

V-4086 WR-1026 (2: 38) **Sophisticated Lady.** **GMMS 37.**
V-4086 WR-1026 (5: 00) Medley: **GMMS 37.**
A Cowboy from Brooklyn.
VR, MH, TB; Int LB.
Call of the Canyon.
VR, RE; Int GM.
V-4086 WR-1026 (3: 06) **Pennsylvania 6-5000.** VR, Band; Int GM. **GMMS 37.**

14 SEPTEMBER 1940.

B Herman "Trigger" Alpert replaces Tony Carlson.

Note:—It appears that although Alpert joined the band on 7 September Carlson did not leave until 13 September (Victor, Nov. '53), so we cannot be certain which bassist is correct for any dates between 7 and 13 September (unless they both "sat in"!). This overlapping of musicians occurs in several instances: where necessary, therefore, a note to this effect has been inserted in this Discography.—*G.E.B.*

19 SEPTEMBER 1940.

Glenn Miller and his Orchestra draw 5000 in St. Louis' Municipal Auditorium.

22 SEPTEMBER 1940—Chesterfield Broadcast.

V-4086 WR-1027 (2: 55) **The gentleman needs a Shave.** VR, MH, TB. **GMMS 38.**
V-4086 WR-1027 (5: 23) Medley: **GMMS 38.**
Isn't it romantic. Int LB.
Shadows on the Sand. VR, RE; Int GM.
Blue Prelude. Int GM.
V-4086 WR-1027 (3: 18) **Tiger Rag.** Int GM, LB. **GMMS 38.**

25 SEPTEMBER 1940—Chesterfield Broadcast.

E1LVB 3200 (2: 49) **Tiger Rag.** **Vi LPT-16,** HMV DLP-1021. Vi 27-0110, Vi 42-0110, Vi 947-0024.

29 SEPTEMBER 1940—Chesterfield Broadcast.

E1LVB 3201 (3: 01) **Everybody loves my baby.** Int GM. **Vi LPT-16,** HMV DLP-1013, Vi 27-0110, Vi 42-0110, Vi 947-0025.

SEPTEMBER 1940—Chesterfield Broadcasts. The exact date of broadcast in September is unknown.

V-4086 WR-1024 (2: 05) **Caprice.** **GMMS 35,** GMMS 83
V-4086 WR-1024 (5: 48) Medley: **GMMS 35,** GMMS 83
Outside of that I love you. VR, MH, TB; Int GM.
Blueberry Hill. VR, RE; Int GM.
V-4086 WR-1024 (4: 13) **Everybody loves my baby.** Int GM. **GMMS 35,** GMMS 83.
V-4086 WR-1025 (2: 04) **In the Gloaming.** Int GM. **GMMS 36,** GMMS 84.
V-4086 WR-1025 (6: 14) Medley: **GMMS 36,** GMMS 84.
Five O'Clock Whistle. VR MH; Int GM.
Trade Winds. VR, MH; Int GM.
V-4086 WR-1025 (3: 18) **Down for the count.** Int GM. **GMMS 36,** GMMS 84.

1 OCTOBER 1940.

Glenn Miller and his Orchestra draws 4000 at the Fernbrook Pavillion, Wilkesbarre, Pennsylvania.

7 OCTOBER 1940.

Glenn Miller and his Orchestra open at the Hotel Pennsylvania in New York.

7 OCTOBER 1940—Chesterfield Broadcast.

V-4086 WR-931 (2: 38) **Sophisticated Lady** **GMMS 1.**
V-4086 WR-931 (2: 03) **Boog Street.** VR, MH, Band; Int GM. **GMMS 1.**
V-4086 WR-931 (3: 00) **April played the fiddle.** VR, RE; Int GM. **GMMS 1.**
V-4086 WR-931 (2: 05) **Tiger Rag.** Int GM. **GMMS 1.**

11 OCTOBER 1940—Victor recording session.

VR Add Paula Kelly and the Modernaires (4M).
(Modernaires: Bill Conway, Hal Dickinson, Ralph Brewster, and Chuck Goldstein).

Note:—Paula Kelly is the wife of Hal Dickinson.

Note:—The Modernaires were hired for this one session: they joined the band permanently later.—*G.E.B.*

056479 **Make Believe Ballroom Time.** VR, 4M. **BB 10913,** HMV 7EG8077, ViJ 1101.
056480 **You've got me this way.** VR, RE. **BB 10906,** HMV BD5670.
056481 **A Nightingale Sang in Berkeley Square.** VR, RE. **BB 10931,** HMV BD5850, HMV MH142, HMV DLP 1049, HMVSw JK-2354. .
056482 **I'd know you anywhere.** VR, RE. **BB 10906,** HMV BD5670.

Note:—The personnel of the trumpet section is a little complicated at this period. The section at the 11 October session was Frankhauser, McMickle, Best and Zarchey; Phil Rommel came in at this period (on October 12 according to Victor (Nov. '53)) and Zarchey left on the 18th. Max Kaminsky came in on the 19th, so for the broadcast of 23 October the section could have been any four of Frankhauser, McMickle, Best, Rommel and Kaminsky (or perhaps all five), and, similarly for the broadcast of 25 October, which was also the date of Rommel's departure.

On 7 November Frankhauser and Kaminsky left, having been replaced by Billy May and Ray Anthony who had joined on 1 November (all dates according to Victor (Nov. '53)).—*G.E.B.*

18 OCTOBER 1940.

Glenn Miller and his Orchestra draw 5200 in Rochester, New York.

23 OCTOBER 1940—Chesterfield broadcast.

E4VP 8210 (2: 35) **On the Alamo.** **Vi GMLE 2.**

25 OCTOBER 1940—Café Rouge, Hotel Pennsylvania, broadcast.

E4VP 8202 (2: 10) **Crosstown.** VR, JL. **Vi GMLE 2.**

Note:—According to Victor (Jan. '55) the trumpets on the 25th October broadcast were Frankhauser, McMickle, Best and Kaminsky, but this contradicts their Nov. '53 information. However, in their Jan. '55 listing they omit Rommel entirely, although it is known that he definitely played in the Band at this period (*see* "Metronome," November 1940).—*G.E.B.*

8 NOVEMBER 1940—Victor recording session.

TB Glenn Miller, Jimmy Priddy, Paul Tanner, Frank D'Annolfo;
TP R. Dale McMickle, John Best, Billy May, Ray Anthony;
S Hal McIntyre AS, Willie Schwartz AS & Clar, Tex Beneke TS, Al Klink TS, Ernie Caceres AS & BS;
Rh J. C. "Chummy" MacGregor P; Herman "Trigger" Alpert B; Jack Lathrop G; Maurice Purtill D.
VR Marion Hutton, Ray Eberle, Tex Beneke, Ernie Caceres, Jack Lathrop.

057610 **Fresh as a Daisy.** VR, MH, JL, TB. **BB 10959,** HMV MH95, HMVAu EA-3345, HMVSw JK-2269.
057611 **Isn't that just like love.** VR, JL. **BB 10936.**
057612 **Along the Santa Fe Trail.** VR, RE. **BB 10970,** HMVAu EA-2787, HMVSw JK-2199, Vi 20-1529.
057613 **Do you know why?** VR, RE. **BB 10936.**

15 NOVEMBER 1940—Victor recording session.

057648 **Somewhere.** VR, RE. **BB 10959,** HMVAu EA-2880, HMVSw JK-2269.
057649 **Yes my darling daughter.** VR, MH. **BB 10970,** HMV BD5683, HMV MH140 HMVAu EA-2787, HMVSw JK-2199.

16 NOVEMBER 1940—Café Rouge, Hotel Pennsylvania, broadcast.

E4VP 8201 (2: 05) **Isn't that just like love.** VR, JL. **Vi GMLE 2.**

18 NOVEMBER 1940—Café Rouge, Hotel Pennsylvania, broadcast.

E4VP 8201 (4: 00) **In a sentimental mood** **Vi GMLE 2.**

20 NOVEMBER 1940.

Glenn Miller and his Orchestra broadcast from the Hotel Pennsylvania, 11.30 p.m.: Lights Out. VR, MH/ Hold Tight, Hold Tight. VR, MH/ Do you know why. VR, RE/ A Million Dreams Ago. VR, RE/ Isn't that just like love. VR, JL/ St. Louis Blues/ Oh So Good.

22 NOVEMBER 1940—Victor recording session.

057661 **Stone's throw from Heaven.** VR, RE **BB 11063.**
057662 **Helpless.** VR, RE. **Vi 20-1600.**
057663 **Long time no see baby.** VR, MH. **Vi 20-1563.**
057664 **You are the one.** VR, RE. **BB 11020.**

22 NOVEMBER 1940—Café Rouge, Hotel Pennsylvania, broadcast.

E4VP 8201 (3: 01) **Along the Santa Fe Trail.** VR, RE. **Vi GMLE 2.**

23 NOVEMBER 1940—Café Rouge, Hotel Pennsylvania, broadcast.

E4VP 8202 (2: 35) **A Million Dreams Ago.** VR, RE. **Vi GMLE 2.**

4 DECEMBER 1940—Chesterfield Broadcast.

E2VL 4420 (2: 52) **Limehouse Blues** **Vi LPT-30,** HMV DLP-1012, Vi 27-0154, Vi 42-0154, Vi 947-0027.

7 DECEMBER 1940.

Glenn Miller and his Orchestra draw 2005 at Youngstown, Ohio.

13 DECEMBER 1940—Victor recording session.

058172 **Anvil Chorus,** Part 1. **BB 10982,**
HMV BD5671, HMV MH183, HMVAu EA-2911,
Vi 20-1495, ViJ 1082.

058173 **Anvil Chorus,** Part 2. **BB 10982,**
HMV BD5671, HMV MH183, HMVAu EA-2911,
Vi 20-1495, ViJ 1082.

Note:—This was the sixth and final time that "Anvil Chorus" was cut—Glenn was finally satisfied. Victor may have issued various takes on some of their re-issues.

058174 **Frenesi.** **BB 10994,**
HMV BD5678, HMVSw JK-2323, ViJ 1099.

E2VL 4547 **Anvil Chorus.** **Vi LPT-3002,**
(Dubbed complete from 058172 and 058173)
Vi 947-0038, HMV DLP1081.

17 DECEMBER 1940—Chesterfield broadcast (Café Rouge, Hotel Pennsylvania).

E3VP 5242 (1: 40) **Fresh as a daisy.** VR, MH, **Vi GMLE.**
TB JL.

E4VP 8202 (4: 20) **Daisy Mae.** **Vi GMLE 2.**

E4VP 8202 (3: 25) **Falling Leaves.** **Vi GMLE 2.**

18 DECEMBER 1940—Chesterfield broadcast.

E1VLB 3200 (2: 17) **Going Home.** **Vi LPT-16,**
Vi 27-0108, Vi 42-0108, Vi 947-0024.

19 DECEMBER 1940—Chesterfield broadcast.

E3VP 5245 (1: 43) **Under a blanket of blue** **Vi GMLE.**

21 DECEMBER 1940—Café Rouge, Hotel Pennsylvania, broadcast.

E4VP 8202 (2: 40) **Are You Jumping Jack.** **Vi GMLE 2.**

24 DECEMBER 1940.

Glenn Miller and his Orchestra break all records at Harlem's famed Savoy.

27 DECEMBER 1940—Victor recording session.

058805 **Memory of a rose,** VR, RE. **BB 11011.**

058806 **I Do, Do You?** VR, RE. **BB 11020.**

058807 **Chapel in the Valley.** VR, RE. **BB 11029.**
HMV MH102, HMVSw JK-2324.

058808 **Prairieland Lullaby.** VR, RE. **BB 11011.**
HMVAu EA-3556.

28 DECEMBER 1940—Café Rouge, Hotel Pennsylvania, broadcast.

E4VP 8202 (3: 25) **You walked by.** VR, RE. **Vi GMLE 2.**

E4VP 8201 (4: 45) **I Dreamt I dwelt in Harlem** **Vi GMLE 2.**

1940—Chesterfield Broadcasts.

The following are selections taken from the Chesterfield broadcasts of 1940. The exact date of broadcast in 1940 is unknown.

V-4086 WR-1105 (2: 30) **Rug Cutter's Swing.** **GMMS 43.**
V-4086 WR-1105 (4: 45) Medley: **GMMS 43.**
Boog it. VR, MH.
When the swallows come back to Capistrano. VR, RE; Int GM.
V-4086 WR-1105 (3: 00) **My Blue Heaven.** Int GM. **GMMS 43.**
V-4086 WR-1109 (1: 45) **Largo.** **GMMS 51.**
V-4086 WR-1109 (5: 58) Medley: **GMMS 51.**
Poor Butterfly. Int GM., LB.
The Sky Fell Down. VR, RE; Int GM.
I'm getting sentimental over You. Int LB; Solo: TB Section.
Black and Blue. Int LB.
V-4086 WR-1109 (3: 20) **Slip Horn Jive.** Int, GM, LB. **GMMS 51.**
V-4086 WR-1111 (3: 08) **Conversation Piece.** **GMMS 46.**
V-4086 WR-1111 (4: 12) Medley: **GMMS 46.**
When you wish upon a star. VR, RE; Int GM.
Be Happy. VR, MH; Int GM.
V-4086 WR-1111 (3: 32) **String of Pearls.** **GMMS 46.**
V-4086 WR-1112 (2: 30) **T'aint no use at all.** **GMMS 44.**
V-4086 WR-1112 (5: 40) Medley: **GMMS 44.**
Goodnight Sweetheart. Int GM.
I'm stepping out with a memory Tonight. VR, RE; Int GM.
When my baby smiles at me. Int LB.
A Blues Serenade. Int LB.
V-4086 WR-1112 (3: 15) **Bugle Call Rag.** Int GM. **GMMS 44.**
V-4086 WR-1113 (2: 30) **I guess I'll have to change my plan.** VR, MH, TB. **GMMS 41.**
V-4086 WR-1113 (5: 00) Medley: **GMMS 41.**
My Darling. Int GM.
Blueberry Hill. VR, RE; Int GM.
I can't get started. Int GM.
Blue. Int LB.
V-4086 WR-1113 (3: 08) **Sliphorn Jive.** Int. GM. **GMMS 41.**

7 January 1941—Broadcast (? Sunset Serenade).

V-4086 WR-981 (1: 45) **Largo.** **GMMS 21,** GMMS 69.
V-4086 WR-981 (5: 33) Medley: **GMMS 21,** GMMS 69.
Bugle Woogie. VR, MH; Int GM.
(Dedicated to the Boys at Shanutt Field, Illinois).
You walked by. VR, RE; Int GM.
V-4086 WR-981 (3: 30) **Oh so good.** VR, Band. **GMMS 21,** GMMS 69.
V-4086 WR-986 (2: 34) **On the Alamo.** **GMMS 26,** GMMS 74.

V-4086 WR-986 (4: 15) Medley: **GMMS 26,** GMMS 74.
A love song hasn't been sung.
VR, RE; Int GM.
A little bit south of North Carolina. VR, PK; Int GM.
(Dedicated to the Boys at the Charlotte Army Base).

V-4086 WR-986 (4: 02) **Here we go again.** **GMMS 26,** GMMS 74.

11 January 1941—Café Rouge, Hotel Pennsylvania, broadcast.

E4VP 8201 (3: 10) **Swinging at the Seance.** **Vi GMLE 2.**
VR, MH. Featuring Billy May, TP.

E4VP 8201 (3: 50) **Frenesi.** **Vi GMLE 2.**

15 January 1941

VR Modernaires (4M) group joined the Band permanently.

15 January 1941—Chesterfield Broadcast.

VR Dorothy Claire replaces Marion Hutton.

E3VP 5244 (2: 08) **Naughty Sweetie Blues.** **Vi GMLE.**
VR DC.

17 January 1941—Victor recording session.

058884 **Ida.** VR TB. **BB 11079,**
HMV DLP 1062, HMVAu EA-3253, Vi 20-2510, Vi GMLE, Vi LPT-3067, Vi EPBT-3067.

058885 **Song of the Volga Boatmen.** **BB 11029,**
HMV BD-5798, HMV MH-138, HMV DLP1062, HMVSw JK-2324, Vi 20-1564, Vi 27-0004, Vi 47-2852, Vi EPA-148, Vi LPT-2, Vi LPM 31, Vi LPT 3067, Vi 47-2877, Vi EPBT-3067.

058886 **The one I love.** VR, RE, 4M. **BB 11110,**
HMV BD-5698, HMVSw JK-2325.

058887 **You stepped out of a dream** VR, RE. **BB 11042.**

058888 **I dreamt I dwelt in Harlem.** **BB 11063,**
HMV BD-5817, HMV MH-143, HMVAu EA-2988

058889 **Sun Valley Jump.** **BB 11110,**
HMV BD-5817, HMV MH-143, HMVAu EA-2863 HMVSw JK-2304, Vi GMLE.

30 January 1941—Chesterfield Broadcast.

E3VP 5240 (2: 55) **There'll be some changes made.** VR, DC. **Vi GMLE.**

February 1941.

Glenn Miller signs a contract with RCA Victor for $750.00 per selection plus royalties.

19 FEBRUARY 1941—Victor recording session.

060911 **When that man is dead and gone.** VR, DC, TB, 4M. **BB 11069,** HMVSw JK-2304.

060912 **The Spirit is Willing.** **BB 11135,** HMV 7EG 8031, HMV Au EA-2863, Vi LPT-1031, Vi EPAT-428.

060913 **Little old church in England.** VR, DC, RE, 4M. **BB 11069,** HMV MH-102.

060914 **Perfidia.** VR, DC, 4M. **BB 11095,** HMV BD-5698, HMV DLP 1049, HMVSw JK-2268, Vi 20-2412, Vi 27-0157, Vi 42-0157, VdP AV-695, Vi LPT-1016, Vi EPAT-430.

20 FEBRUARY 1941—Victor recording session.

060915 **It's Always You.** VR, RE. **BB 11079,** HMVSw JK-2252.

060916 **Spring will be so sad.** VR, RE, 4M. **BB 11095,** HMVSw JK-2268, VdP AV-695.

060917 **The Air Minded Executive.** VR, DC, TB. **BB 11135.**

060918 **Below the Equator.** VR, RE, 4M. **BB 11235,** HMVAu EA-2931

MARCH 1941—Hollywood.

VR *Add* Paula Kelly.

20th Century Fox produces the film "SUN VALLEY SERENADE."

The picture stars Sonja Henie, John Payne, Milton Berle, Lynn Bari, Joan Davis, the Nicholas Brothers, and Glenn Miller and His Orchestra. Lorraine Elliot does the vocal selections for Lynn Bari.

(1: 15) Introduction.
(0: 47) Moonlight Serenade.
(4: 38) I know why—VR LE, John Payne.
(0: 34) The Farmer in the Dell.
(3: 19) In The Mood.
(2: 09) It happened in Sun Valley. VR, PK, RE, TB, EC, 4M.
(7: 29) Chattanooga Choo Choo. VR, PK, TB, 4M, Nicholas Bros. & Dorothy Dandridge.
(2: 00) Kiss Polka. VR, Sonja Henie, John Payne.
(1: 45) I know why. VR, Sonja Henie, John Payne.
(7: 37) Choral Selections: Kiss Polka, It happened in Sun Valley.
"Mood" Music—Throughout the 1½ hour film.

MID APRIL 1941—Hollywood.

A fifteen minute radio preview transcription was made of "Sun Valley Serenade." None of the selections were taken from the sound track.

Moonlight Serenade.
I Know Why. VR, PK, RE, 4M.
In The Mood.
It happened in Sun Valley. VR, PK, RE, TB, EC, 4M.
Chattanooga Choo Choo. VR, TB, 4M.

In September 1954 R.C.A. Victor released a ten inch L.P. containing selections from the sound track of "Sun Valley Serenade." Very few of these selections were actually put in the film soundtracks—the Victor issues were probably alternative takes of the film recordings.

E4VL 5049 (2: 12) **It happened in Sun Valley.** VR, 4M, Band. **Vi LPT 3064,** Vi 947-0201, EPBT3064, HMV DLP1104.

E4VL 5049 (3: 12) **In the Mood.** **Vi LPT 3064,** Vi EPBT 3064, Vi 947-0201, HMV DLP1104.

E4VL 5049 (4: 56) **At Last.** VR, John Payne, LE. **Vi LPT 3064,** Vi EPBT 3064, Vi 947-0202, HMV DLP1104.

E4VL 5049 (7: 42) **Chattanooga Choo Choo.** VR, PK, TB, 4M, Nicholas Brothers, Dorothy Dandridge. **Vi LPT 3064,** Vi EPBT 3064, Vi 947-0202, HMV DLP1104.

E4VL 5050 (4: 31) **I Know Why.** VR, 4M, LE, John Payne. **Vi LPT 3064,** Vi EPBT 3064, Vi 947-0201, HMV DLP1104.

E4VL 5050 (2: 26) **Sun Valley Jump.** **Vi LPT 3064,** Vi EPBT 3064, Vi 947-0201, HMV DLP1104.

E4VL 5050 (2: 35) **Measure for Measure.** **Vi LPT 3064.** HMV DLP1104.

E4VL 5050 (3: 24) **Spirit is willing.** **Vi LPT 3064.** HMV DLP1104.

It is interesting to note that not one vocal credit appears anywhere on either the record or the sleeve.

Note:—"Sun Valley Jump," "Measure for Measure" and "The Spirit is Willing," although not used in the completed film, were nevertheless recorded at the time specially for the film.—*G.E.B.*

30 April 1941—Chesterfield Broadcast.

E3VP 5245 (1: 47) **Just a little bit south of North Carolina.** VR, DC. **Vi GMLE.**

7 May 1941—Hollywood, Victor recording session.

VR Dorothy Claire *out.*

061246 **Boulder Buff.** **BB 11163,** HMV BD-5711, HMVAu EA-2988, Vi GMLE.

061244 **Booglie Wooglie Piggy.** VR, TB, 4M. **BB 11163,** HMV BD-5711, HMVAu EA-2882.

061245 **Chattanooga Choo Choo.** VR, TB, PK, 4M. **BB 11230,** HMV BD-5720, HMV DLP-1024, HMVF 7EMF11, HMVAu EA-2999, HMVSw JK-2357, Vi 20-2410, Vi 27-0026, Vi 42-0026, Vi 47-2858, Vi EPA-529, Vi EPAT-401, Vi LPT 1016, Vi 20-2972.

061246 **I Know Why.** VR, PK, 4M. **BB 11230,** HMV BD-5720, HMV DLP-1024, HMVSw JK-2357.

20 May 1941—Hollywood, Victor recording session.

TP Harry Geller, replaces John Best.

061253 **Don't Cry Cherie.** VR, RE. **BB 11183,**
HMV MH-93, HMVAu EA-2872,

061254 **Cradle Song.** VR, RE, Choir. **BB 11203,**
HMV BD-5733, HMV MH-137.

061255 **Sweeter than the Sweetest.** **BB 11183,** HMV MH-93.
VR, PK, 4M.

Note:—There is some uncertainty regarding the guitarist and the bassist at this period. Jack Lathrop left on 22 May and his permanent successor, Bobby Hackett, didn't join until 10 July. From 23 May to 9 July the guitarist was almost certainly Bill Conway of the Modernaires singing group. Photographs and other information support this.

Bassist "Trigger" Alpert left on 13 June and his permanent successor Edward "Doc" Goldberg didn't join until 20 June, but on 13 June a certain M. Rubin (instrument unknown) joined and stayed until 26 June (all dates according to Victor (Nov. '53). Rubin *may* have been the bassist between Alpert's departure and Goldberg's entry, also staying on during Goldberg's first week.—*G.E.B.*

28 May 1941—Hollywood, Victor recording session.

TP John Best replaces Harry Geller.

061265 **I guess I'll have to dream the rest.** **BB 11187,** HMV 7EG8097.
VR, RE, 4M.

061266 **Take the "A" Train.** **BB 11187,** HMV BD-5829.
HMV 7EG8031, Vi LPT-1031, Vi EPAT-428.

061267 **Peek-a-boo to you.** VR, 4M. **BB 11203.**

061268 **Angels Came Through.** VR, RE. **BB 11215.**

11 June 1941—Chesterfield Broadcast.

V-4086 WR-985 (4: 58) Medley: **GMMS 25,** GMMS 73.
Whatcha Know Joe.
VR, TB, Band.
Dancing in a Dream.
VR, RE; Int GM.

V-4086 WR-985 (2: 14) **Boog It.** VR, MH. **GMMS 25,** GMMS 73.

V-4086 WR-985 (3: 17) **Are You Rusty, Gate?** **GMMS 25,** GMMS 73.
Int GM; Clt & AS, Ernie Caceres.

25 June 1941—Chicago, Victor recording session.

TB Warren Smith, replaces Frank D'Annolfo;
B Doc Goldberg replaces Herman "Trigger" Alpert;
G Bill Conway, replaces Jack Lathrop;

064471 **Under Blue Canadian Skies.** VR, RE. **BB 11219,**
HMV BD-5727, HMVAu EA-3484.

064472 **Cowboy Serenade.** VR, RE. **BB 11235,** HMV JO-198.

064473 **You and I.** VR, RE. **BB 11215,** HMV JO-198.

064474 **Adios.** **BB 11219,**
AFR 50, HMV BD-5727, HMV DLP1081, Vi 20-2942, Vi 947-0039, Vi LPT-3002.

25 June 1941—Chesterfield broadcast.

E2VL 4545 (2: 45) **Are You Rusty Gate?**
a Jerry Gray **Vi LPT-3001,**
HMV DLP 1021, Vi 947-0054.

26 June 1941—Chesterfield broadcast.

E4VP 8210 (1: 50) **Dancing in a Dream.** **Vi GMLE 2.**
VR, RE.

Glenn Miller and his Orchestra playing at the Hotel Pennsylvania, New York, early in 1940. Personnel (left to right): Leigh Knowles, John Best, Dale McMickle, Clyde Hurley (trumpets); Maurice Purtill (drums); Roland Bundock (bass); Paul Tanner, Jimmy Priddy, Frank D'Annolfo, Glenn Miller (trombones); Al Klink, Willie Schwartz, Hal McIntyre, Ernie Caceres, Tex Beneke (saxophones); Guitarist Dick Fisher and pianist Chummy MacGregor are obscured by Miller. Seated at the left is singer Ray Eberle.

The Glenn Miller singers Ray Eberle (centre), Marion Hutton, and the Modernaires, during an engagement at the Hotel Pennsylvania in 1941. The Modernaires are (left to right): Bill Conway, Hal Dickenson, Chuck Goldstein and Ralph Brewster.

27 JUNE 1941.

TB Frank D'Annolfo replaces Warren Smith.

29 JUNE 1941—Chesterfield broadcast.

Glenn Miller and his Orchestra feature a "red-hot" arrangement of "Swing Low Sweet Chariot."

1 JULY 1941—Chesterfield broadcast.

E4VP 8207 (2: 00) **I don't want to walk without You.** **Vi GMLE 2.**
VR, probably Skip Nelson (not RE as given in Vi Album).

3 JULY 1941—Chesterfield broadcast from the Pacific Square, San Diego, California.

E3VP 5236 (4: 09) **Perfidia.** VR, PK, 4M; Int GM. **Vi GMLE.**

9 JULY 1941—Chesterfield broadcast.

TP Alec Fila replaces Ray Anthony.

E2VL 4546 (3: 45) **Intermezzo.** a Bill Finegan **Vi LPT-3001,** HMV DLP 1021, Vi 947-0055.

Note:—According to Victor (Nov. '53) Alec Fila joined on 4 July and Ray Anthony left on 11 July—thus either (or both?) could have played on this broadcast.—*G.E.B.*

10 JULY 1941.

G Bobby Hackett joins the Band (*see also Note* on page 52). Hackett also played featured cornet and trumpet solos in some numbers.

16 JULY 1941—broadcast.

E3VP 5243 (2: 50) **Twenty-four Robbers.** **Vi GMLE.**
VR, PK, TB, 4M; Int I.B.

11 AUGUST 1941—New York, Victor recording session.

TB Glenn Miller, Jimmy Priddy, Frank D'Annolfo, Paul Tanner;
TP R. Dale McMickle, John Best, Alec Fila, Billy May;
S Hal McIntyre AS, Willie Schwartz AS & Clt, Tex Beneke TS, Al Klink TS, Ernie Caceres BS & AS;
Rh J. C. "Chummy" MacGregor P; Edward "Doc" Goldberg B; Bobby Hackett G & TP; Maurice Purtill D.
VR Paula Kelly, Ray Eberle, Tex Beneke, Four Modernaires, Ernie Caceres.

067625 **It happened in Sun Valley.** **BB 11263,** HMV MH17.
VR, PK, RE, TB, EC, 4M.

067626 **I'm Thrilled.** VR, RE. **BB 11287.**
C solo Bobby Hackett.

067627 **The Kiss Polka.** VR, PK, EC, 4M; **BB 11263,** HMV MH17.
Maraccas, RE.

067628 **Delilah.** VR, TB, 4M. **BB 11274,**
HMV BD1216, HMV DLP 1062, Vi 20-2942, Vi EPBT 3067, Vi LPT-3067, Vi EPAT 429.

067629 **From one love to another.** VR, RE. **BB 11287,** HMVAu EA-3139
C solo Bobby Hackett.

067630 **Elmer's Tune.** VR, RE, 4M. **BB 11274,**
HMV BD5733, HMV MH137, HMVAu EA-2999, Vi 20-3185, Vi LPT-1016, Vi EPAT 429.

13 August 1941—Chesterfield broadcast.

E1VLB 3201 (3: 36) **Georgia on my mind.** **Vi LPT-16,**
HMV B10235, HMV DLP 1013, Vi 27-0109,
Vi 42-0109, Vi 947-0025.

3 September 1941—Victor recording session.

VR Marion Hutton replaces Paula Kelly.

067741 **Says who, says you, says I.** **BB 11315,**
VR, MH, TB. HMVAu EA-2940.
067742 **Orange Blossom Lane.** VR, RE. **BB 11326.**
067743 **Dear Arabella.** VR, MH, TB, 4M. **BB 11326.**
067744 **Man in the moon.** VR, RE. **BB 11299.**
067745 **Ma-Ma-Maria.** VR, RE, 4M. **BB 11299,** HMV MH-99.
067746 **This time the dream's on me.** **BB 11315.**
VR, RE.

5 September 1941—Chesterfield Broadcast.

E3VP 5240 (3: 50) **Oh So Good.** VR, Band; **Vi GMLE.**
Int GM.

6 October 1941

Glenn Miller and his Orchestra open at the Hotel Pennsylvania in New York.

16 October 1941—Chesterfield Broadcast.

AS Benny Feman replaces Hal McIntyre.

E2VL 4420 (2: 32) **Vilia.** **Vi LPT 30,**
HMV MH-172, HMV DLP-1012, Vi 27-0155,
Vi 42-0155, Vi 947-0027.

20 October 1941—Victor recording session.

071190 **Dreamsville Ohio.** VR, RE, 4M. **BB 11342.**
C solo Bobby Hackett.
071191 **Papa Niccolini.** VR, RE, TB, 4M. **BB 11342.**
071192 **Jingle Bells.** VR, TB, EC, 4M. **BB 11353,**
a GM. & Bill Finegan.
AFR-112, HMV BD-5789, HMV MH-57, HMVSw JK-2433, Vi 20-2510.
071193 **This is no laughing matter.** VR, RE. **BB 11369,**
HMV BD-5749, HMV MH-126, HMV DLP 1049.

3 November 1941—Victor recording session.

S Irving "Babe" Russin replaces Benny Feman.

068066 **Humpty Dumpty Heart.** VR, RE. **BB 11369,**
HMV BD-5749, HMV MH-126.
068067 **Everything I love.** VR, RE, Choir. **BB 11365.**
068068 **String of Pearls.** **BB 11382,**
C solo Bobby Hackett.
HMV BD-5927, HMV DLP-1024, HMVSw JK-2412, Vi 20-1552, Vi 20-4086, Vi 27-0085, Vi 47-2858, Vi 47-4086, Vi 947-0090, Vi LPT-12, Vi LPT-3036.
068069 **Baby Mine.** VR, RE, Choir. **BB 11365.**

068070 **Long Tall Mama.** **Vi 27943,**
C Bobby Hackett; TP Billy May.
HMV 7EG8031, Vi LPT 1031, Vi EPAT-428.

068071 **Day Dreaming.** VR, RE. **BB 11382.**

Note:—Beneke was reported to have played lead alto at this session—thus the tenors would be Russin and Klink.—*G.E.B.*

Note:—Some chopping and changing seems to have occurred in the trumpet section during the period November 1941 to January 1942: Alec Fila left on 13 November (he joined the Goodman band in exchange for Lloyd "Skippy" Martin who joined Glenn Miller as lead alto on 14 November), and following this Reuben "Zeke" Zarchey came in for three separate periods—21 to 27 November, 5 to 18 December, and 2 to 8 January. Permanent replacement for Fila was Steve Lipkins who joined on 21 January 1942 (all dates by Victor (Nov. '53)). In the periods between Zarchey's spells with the band, and until Lipkins joined, the fourth trumpet was (sometimes at least) Bobby Hackett. When Hackett played in the trumpet section, his place on guitar was usually taken by Bill Conway (of the Modernaires vocal group).—*G.E.B.*

22 November 1941.

Glenn Miller and his Orchestra were featured on "Coke's Spotlight Bands' broadcast.

24 November 1941—Victor recording session.

TP Reuben "Zeke" Zarchey replaces Alec Fila;
S Lloyd "Skippy" Martin replaces Irving "Babe" Russin.

068240 **(There'll be bluebirds over) The White Cliffs of Dover.** VR, RE. **BB 11397,** **HMV DLP1049.**

068241 **We're the Couple in the Castle.** VR, RE. **BB 11397.**

25 November 1941—Chesterfield broadcast.

E3VP 5239 (2: 24) **Bugle Call Rag.** **Vi GMLE.**

1 December 1941—Victor recording session.

TP probably Bobby Hackett replaces Reuben "Zeke" Zarchey.
probably Bill Conway played guitar.

068418 **Moonlight Sonata.** a Bill Finegan. **BB 11386,**
HMV BD5768, HMVSw JK-2338.

068419 **Slumber Song** (The Band's closing theme) **BB 11386,**
HMV BD5768, HMVSw JK-2338.

Note:—At this period, Dean Kincaide joined the Band as arranger—he did not replace anyone. Victor reported (Nov. '53) that he was with the Band from 2 December 1941 to 15 January 1942, and he *may* have deputised on occasion for one of the saxes during this period as well.—*G.E.B.*

6 December 1941—Victor recording session.

TP Reuben "Zeke" Zarchey replaces Bobby Hackett;
G Bobby Hackett replaces Bill Conway.

068442 **It happened in Hawaii.** VR, RE, **4M.** **BB 11416,**
Vi 20-2536, Vi EPAT-430.

8 DECEMBER 1941—Victor recording session.

068456 **Moonlight Cocktail.** VR, RE, 4M. **BB 11401,**
HMV BD-5834, HMVI NE-673, Vi-20-2536, Vi EPA-530, Vi LPT-1016, Vi EPAT-430.

068457 **Happy In Love.** VR, MH. **BB 11401,**
HMVAu EA-3139, HMVI NE-673.

068458 **Fooled.** VR, RE. **BB 11416.**

068459 **Keep 'em flying.** TP Billy May; Clt Ernie Caceres. **BB 11443.**

068460 **Chip off the old block.** **BB 11450,**
HMV BD-5784, HMV MH-141, Vi GMLE.

068461 **Story of a Starry Night.** VR, RE. **BB 11416,**
HMV BD-5768, HMV 7EG8043, HMVAu EA3222 Vi 20-3561, Vi LPT 1031, Vi EPAT-426.

11 DECEMBER 1941—Chesterfield Broadcast.

E3VP 5237 (2: 14) **Introduction to a waltz.** **Vi GMLE.**

25 DECEMBER 1941—Chesterfield Broadcast.

TP probably Bobby Hackett replaces Reuben "Zeke" Zarchey.

E3VP 5242 (3: 25) **Flagwaver.** **Vi GMLE.**

30 DECEMBER 1941—Chesterfield Broadcast.

E3VP 5242 (3: 03) **Chattanooga Choo Choo.** VR, TB, 4M. **Vi GMLE.**

1 JANUARY 1942—Chesterfield broadcast.

E2VL 4419 (3: 41) **I Got Rhythm.** **Vi LPT-30,**
HMV DLP 1012, Vi 27-0154, Vi 42-0154, Vi 947-0026.

5 JANUARY 1942—Victor recording session.

TP Reuben "Zeke" Zarchey joins again.

068833 **At the President's Birthday Ball.** VR, MH, 4M. **BB 11429.**

068834 **Angels of Mercy.** VR, RE, Choir. **BB 11429.**

068835-1 **Dear Mom.** VR, RE, 4M. BB Unissued (reject).

068836 **On the old assembly line.** VR, TB, 4M. **BB 11480.**

068837 **Let's have another cup of coffee.** VR, MH, EC, 4M. **BB 11450,**
HMV BD5784, HMV MH141.

8 JANUARY 1942—Victor recording session.

Note:—There is conflicting evidence as to the fourth trumpet on this session—according to "New Hot Discography" Bill Graham is present, according to Victor it was Reuben "Zeke" Zarchey—unless they were both there and one of McMickle, Best or May were absent!—*G.E.B.*

068789 **Skylark.** VR, RE. **BB 11462.**

068790 **When the roses bloom again.** VR, RE. **BB 11438,** HMV 7EG8097

068791 **Always in my heart.** VR, RE. **BB 11438,**
HMVAu EA-3035, Vi GMLE.

068835-2 **Dear Mom.** (Remake). VR, RE, 4M. **BB 11443,**
HMVAu EA-3167.

10 FEBRUARY 1942—Chesterfield broadcast.

TB Glenn Miller, Jimmy Priddy, Frank D'Annolfo, Paul Tanner;
TP John Best, Steve Lipkins, R. Dale McMickle, Billy May;
S Lloyd "Skippy" Martin AS, Willie Schwartz AS & Clt, Tex Beneke TS, Al Klink TS, Ernie Caceres AS & BS;
(*See* note 6 February 1939 regarding sax section doubling)
Rh J. C. "Chummy" MacGregor P; Edward "Doc" Goldberg B; Bobby Hackett G & TP; Maurice Purtill D.
VR Marion Hutton, Ray Eberle, Tex Beneke, Four Modernaires, Ernie Caceres.

E4VP 8209 (2: 35) **Measure for Measure.** **Vi GMLE 2.**

On this day, Glenn Miller was presented with a gold pressing of "Chatanooga Choo Choo" by the RCA Victor Company. Sales of the recording had just passed the one million mark.

15 FEBRUARY 1942.

Glenn Miller and his Orchestra draw 22,000 in Detroit, Michigan.

16 FEBRUARY 1942.

Glenn Miller and his Orchestra draw 2,000 in London, Ontario, Canada.

17 FEBRUARY 1942.

Glenn Miller and his Orchestra draw 8,000 in Toronto's Mutual Street Arena.

17 FEBRUARY 1942—Toronto, Ontario, Chesterfield broadcast.

E2VL 4420 (2: 52) **On Brave Old Army Team.** **Vi LPT-30,** HMV DLP 1012, Vi 27-0152, Vi 42-0152, Vi 947-0027.

There was trumpet fill-in by a Toronto musician on this date.

18 FEBRUARY 1942—New York, Victor recording session.

071860 **Shh-h-h, it's a Military Secret.** VR, MH, TB, 4M. **BB 11493.**

071861 **Don't sit under the apple tree.** VR, MH, TB, 4M. **BB 11474,** HMV B10662, HMV 7M195, HMV DLP 1062, Vi EPBT 3067, Vi LPT 3067.

071862 **She'll always remember.** VR, RE, 4M. **BB 11493,** HMVAu EA-3337.

071863 **The Lamplighter's Serenade.** VR, RE, 4M. **BB 11474,** Vi GMLE.

071864 **When Johnny comes marching home.** VR, MH, TB, 4M. **BB 11480,** HMV BD5799, HMV MH138, HMVAu EA-3087, Vi 20-1600.

24 FEBRUARY 1942—Chesterfield broadcast.

E2VL 4545 (3: 16) **Tchaikovsky's Piano Concerto.** a Bill Finegan. **Vi LPT-3001,** Vi 947-0054.

26 February 1942—Chesterfield broadcast.

E4VP 8208 (3: 00) **A stone's throw from Heaven.** VR, RE. **Vi GMLE 2.**
E4VP 8210 (2: 15) **V for Victory Hop.** **Vi GMLE 2.**

3 March 1942—Atlantic Spotlight broadcast.

Paula Kelly and the Modernaires were featured singing "Holiday for Strings." Glenn Miller had, by this broadcast, given away 4500 records and 65 console radio-phonographs to the U.S.O.

Note:—According to Victor (Nov. '53) a B. McDevitt (instrument unknown) was with the band from 16 March to 24 May: as this is completely uncorroborated, and it is not readily apparent how he fits into the line-up, we have omitted him altogether.—*G.E.B.*

20 March 1942—Chesterfield broadcast.

E2VL 4546 (2: 28) **Introduction to a waltz.** (Comp. GM, Jerry Gray, Hal Dickenson). **Vi LPT-3001,** HMV DLP 1012, Vi 947-0055.

25 March 1942—Chesterfield broadcast.

E2VL 4419 (1: 58) **Anchors Aweigh.** **Vi LPT-30,** HMV DLP 1012, Vi 947-0026, Vi 27-0152, Vi 42-0152, Vi GMLE 2.

27 March 1942—Chesterfield broadcast.

E4VP 8207 (2: 50) **Limehouse Blues.** **Vi GMLE 2.**
E4VP 8207 (3: 37) **Daddy.** VR, MH, TB, 4M. **Vi GMLE 2.**

2 April 1942—Hollywood, Victor recording session.

072230 **American Patrol.** a Jerry Gray **Vi 27873,** HMV BD5789, HMV BD 5942, HMV MH57, HMV DLP 1021, HMV DLP 1024, HMVAu EA-3253, HMVSw JK-2433, Vi 20-1564, Vi47-2852 Vi EPA-148, Vi LPM-31.
072231 **Soldier, let me read your letter.** VR, RE. **Vi 27873,** HMVAu EA-3175.
072232 **Sleep Song.** VR, RE, 4M. C solo BH. **Vi 27879,** HMV BD5779, HMV MH127.
072233 **Sweet Eloise.** VR, RE, 4M. C BH. **Vi 27879,** HMV BD5779, HMV MH127, HMVAu EA-377, Vi GMLE.

10 April 1942—Chesterfield broadcast.

E3VP 5243 (2: 37) **The Hop.** **Vi GMLE.**
E4VP 8209 (1: 35) **How Deep is the Ocean.** **Vi GMLE 2.**

23 April 1942—Chesterfield broadcast.

E3VP 5239 (2: 45) **American Patrol.** **Vi GMLE.**

LATE APRIL 1942—Hollywood.

20th Century Fox produces the film "ORCHESTRA WIVES."

The picture stars George Montgomery, Carole Landis, Ann Rutherford, Mary Beth Hughes, Cesar Romero, Jimmy Glisson, Lynn Bari, the Nicholas Brothers and Glenn Miller and his Orchestra. Steve Lipkins plays TP for George Montgomery; "Chummy" MacGregor plays Piano for Cesar Romero; "Doc" Goldberg plays Bass for Jimmy Glisson: and Pat Friday does the vocal selections for Lynn Bari.

(0:54) Moonlight Serenade.
(0: 40) Chatanooga Choo Choo.
(3: 40) People like you and me. VR, MH, TB, 4M.
(3: 21) Boom Shot.
(4: 36) At Last. VR, RE, PF.
(0: 52) American Patrol.
(2: 47) Bugle Call Rag.
(2: 57) Serenade in Blue. VR, PF, RE, 4M.
(7: 47) Kalamazoo. VR, MH, TB, 4M, Nicholas Brothers.
"Mood" Music—Throughout the 2-hour film.

EARLY MAY 1942—Hollywood.

A fifteen minute radio preview transcription was made of "Orchestra Wives." None of the selections were taken from the sound track.

(0: 50) **Moonlight Serenade.**
(1: 34) **People like you and me.** VR, MH, 4M.
(1: 48) **At Last.** VR, Lynn Bari, RE.
(1: 48) **Serenade in Blue.** VR, RE, 4M.
(2: 20) **Kalamazoo.** VR, MH, TB, 4M.

Plans were made for the band to return to Hollywood in November 1942, to make the movie "Blind Date."

In September 1954 R.C.A. Victor released a ten inch L.P. containing selections from the soundtrack of "Orchestra Wives." Very few of these selections were actually put in the film soundtracks—the Victor issues were probably alternative takes of the film recordings.

E4VL 5047 (3: 32) **American Patrol.** **Vi LPT-3065,**
Vi EPBT-3065, Vi 947-0203, HMV DLP 1059.

E4VL 5047 (5: 42) **Serenade in Blue.** **Vi LPT-3065,**
VR, PF, RE, 4M.
Vi EPBT-3065, Vi 947-0203, HMV DLP 1059.

E4VP 5047 (2: 35) **That's Sabotage.** VR, MH. **Vi LPT-3065,**
Vi EPBT-3065, Vi 947-0204, HMV DLP 1059.

E4VP 5047 (3: 47) **Moonlight Sonata.** **Vi LPT-3065,**
a B. Finegan.
Vi EPBT-3065, Vi 947-0203, HMV DLP 1059.

E4VP 5048. (8: 33) **Kalamazoo.** VR, MH, TB, **Vi LPT-3065,**
4M, Nicholas Brothers.
Vi EPBT-3065. Vi 947-0204. HMV DLP 1059.

E4VP 5048 (3: 40) **People like you and me.** **Vi LPT-3065,**
VR, MH, RE, TB, 4M.
HMV DLP 1059.

E4VP 5048 (2: 45) **Bugle Call Rag.** **Vi LPT-3065,**
HMV DLP 1059.

It is interesting to note that not one vocal credit appears anywhere on either the record or the sleeve.

Note:—"That's Sabotage" and "Moonlight Sonata," although not used in the completed film (except in some countries, including Canada) were nevertheless recorded at the time specially for the film.—*G.E.B.*

5 MAY 1942—Hollywood, Chesterfield broadcast.

E3VP 5241 (3: 15) **String of Pearls.** **Vi GMLE,** Vi LPT-3057, Vi 947-0137.

7 MAY 1942—Hollywood, Chesterfield Broadcast.

E3VP 5243 (2: 09) **Don't sit under the apple Tree.** VR, MH, TB, 4M. **Vi GMLE.**

15 MAY 1942—Hollywood.

Glenn Miller and his Orchestra draw 7,300 at the Hollywood Palladium.

18 MAY 1942—Chesterfield broadcast, Hollywood.

E4VP 8207 (2: 35) **Deep in the heart of Texas.** VR, MH, TB, 4M. **Vi GMLE 2.**

20 MAY 1942—Hollywood, Victor recording session.

072283 **Kalamazoo.** VR, MH, TB, 4M. **Vi 27934,** HMV BD5808, HMVAu EA-3171, HMVF 7EMF11, HMVSw JK-2422, Vi 27-0026, Vi 42-0026, Vi EPAT-401, Vi LPT-1016, Vi EPA 530.

072284 **Serenade in Blue.** VR, RE, 4M. C solo Bobby Hackett. **Vi 27935,** HMV BD5808, HMVAu EA-3171, HMVSw JK-2329, HMVI NE-651, Vi 20-2889, VdP AV-721, Vi LPT-1016, Vi EPAT-430.

072285 **At Last.** VR, RE. **Vi 27934,** HMV BD5811, HMV DLP 1024, HMVAu EA3711 HMVSw JK-2329, Vi 27-0157, Vi 42-0157, Vi EPAT-429, Vi LPT-1016, V-D 12.

072286 **Lullaby of the rain.** VR, RE, 4M. **Vi 27894.**

072287 **Knit one purl two.** VR, MH, 4M. **Vi 27894.**

26 MAY 1942

Glenn Miller's "Sunset Serenade" switches to the CBS Network.

28 MAY 1942—Chesterfield Broadcast.

E2VL 4546 (2: 13) **Sleepy Lagoon.** a Bill Finegan. **Vi LPT-3001,** HMV DLP-1013, Vi 947-0055.

30 MAY 1942—Kansas City.

Glenn Miller and his Orchestra draw 9,005 at Kansas City's Municipal Auditorium.

3 JUNE 1942—Chesterfield Broadcast.

E1LVB 3201 (2: 10) **Jersey Bounce.** **Vi LPT-16,** HMV B-10235, HMV DLP-1013, Vi 27-0108, Vi 42-0108, Vi 947-0025.

17 June 1942—New York, Victor recording session.

075090 **That's Sabotage.** VR, MH. **Vi 27935,**
HMVAu EA-3175, HMVI NE-651, VdP AV-721.

075091 **Conchita, Marquita, Lolita, Pepita,** **Vi 27943.**
Roseta, Juanita, Lopez.
VR, MH, TB, EC, 4M.

075092 **The Humming Bird.** VR, MH, TB, **Vi 27933,**
4M. HMVAu EA-3191.

075093 **Yesterday's Gardenias.** VR, RE, 4M, **Vi 27933.**

Note:—Victor reported (Nov. '53) that a G. Kunstmann (instrument unknown) was with the band from 30 June to 27 August: as this is completely uncorroborated, and it is not readily apparent how he fits into the lineup, we have omitted him altogether.—*G.E.B.*

14 July 1942—Chicago, Victor recording session.

VR Skip Nelson, replaces Richard "Ray" Eberle.

074736 **Dearly Beloved.** VR, SN. **Vi 27953,**

074737 **Moonlight Mood.** VR, 4M. **Vi 20-1520,**
HMVAu EA-3057, HMV 7EG8077, V-D 12.

074738 **Caribbean Clipper.** TP, Billy May; **Vi 20-1536,**
TS Al Klink HMV BD-5833, Vi GMLE.

074739 **Here we go again.** **Vi 20-1563,**
HMV 7EG 8077, Vi GMLE.

074740 **That Old Black Magic.** VR, SN, 4M. **Vi 20-1523,**
HMV BD-5811, HMVF 7EMF 11, HMVSw JK-2326, Vi 20-1560, Vi 27-0035, Vi 27-0089, Vi 42-0089, Vi EPAT-401, Vi LPT-1016, Vi LPT-12

15 July 1942—Chicago, Victor recording session.

074741 **Moonlight Becomes You.** VR, SN, **Vi 20-1520,**
4M. HMVAu EA-3035, HMV 7EG 8067, Vi LPT-1016, Vi EPAT-427.

074742 **Juke Box Saturday Night.** **Vi 20-1509,**
VR, MH, TB, 4M.
HMV BD-5876, HMVAu EA-3036, HMVF 7EMF 11, Vi 20-3185, Vi 27-0035, Vi 42-0035, Vi EPAT-401, Vi LPT-1016.

074743 **It must be Jelly.** VR, 4M. **Vi 20-1546,**
a George Williams.
HMV BD-5847, HMVSw JK-2339.

074744 **I'm Old Fashioned.** VR, SN. **Vi 27953.**

074745 **Pink Cocktail for a Blue Lady.** **Vi 20-1523.**
VR, SN.

16 July 1942—Chicago, Victor recording session.

074746 **Rainbow Rhapsody.** C, B. Hackett. **Vi 20-1546,**
HMV BD-5847, HMV 7EG8031, HMVSw JK-2339 Vi LPT-1031, Vi EPAT-428, Vi GMLE.

074747 **Sleepy Town Train.** **Vi 20-1509,**
HMV BD-5876, HMVAu EA-3063, HMVSw JK-2396, VD 201, Vi GMLE.

074748 **Rhapsody in Blue.** **Vi 20-1529,**
HMV BD-5832, HMVAu EA-3222, Vi GMLE.

Note:—Owing to a dispute between the American Federation of Musicians and the recording companies, a recording ban was imposed by the Union on its members as from August 1, 1942; this session, therefore, was the last by the Miller band.—*G.E.B.*

19 AUGUST 1942—Chesterfield Broadcast.

E2VL 4419 (2: 31) **My Buddy** **Vi LPT-30,**
HMV DLP 1012, Vi 27-0153, Vi 42-0153, Vi 947-0026.

25 AUGUST 1942—Chesterfield broadcast.

E4VP 8209 (3: 01) **Let's have another cup of coffee.** VR, MH, EC, 4M. **Vi GMLE 2.**

1 SEPTEMBER 1942—Chesterfield broadcast.

E4VP 8210 (2: 25) **April in Paris.** **Vi GMLE 2.**
a Bill Finegan.

9 SEPTEMBER 1942—Chesterfield broadcast.

E3VP 5237 (2: 00) **Make Believe.** **Vi GMLE.**
E3VP 5242 (1: 58) **My Devotion.** VR, SN, 4M. **Vi GMLE.**

15 SEPTEMBER 1942—Chesterfield Broadcast.

E3VP 5238 (3: 20) **It must be Jelly.** VR, Band **Vi GMLE.**

22 SEPTEMBER 1942—Chesterfield Broadcast.

E2VL 4545 (2: 25) **April in Paris.** **Vi LPT-3001,**
a Bill Finegan.
HMV DLP 1021, Vi 947-0054.

26 SEPTEMBER 1942—Coke Spotlight Band Review.

This was the last "Coke" broadcast featuring Glenn Miller and his Orchestra. It was aired from the Central Theatre in Passaic, New Jersey.

29 SEPTEMBER 1942—Chesterfield Broadcast.

This was the final Chesterfield Programme. It was aired from the Central Theatre in Passaic New Jersey. This was the band's last performance.

(2: 38) In the Mood.
(2: 31) Kalamazoo. VR, MH, TB, 4M.
(3: 07) Juke Box Saturday Night. VR, MH, TB, 4M.
Featuring Harry James TP.

Glenn Miller disbands the Orchestra to accept a Captain's Commission in the United States Army Air Force.

The following are air checks taken from some of the broadcasts made in 1942. The date of broadcast is unknown.

(2: 31) Bugle Call Rag.
(2: 12) Caribbean Clipper.
(1: 53) I've Caught Love. VR, SN, 4M.
(2: 13) Jersey Bounce.
(1: 31) Jingle Jangle Jingle.
(4: 11) Kalamazoo. VR, MH, TB, 4M.
(2: 01) My Devotion. VR, SN, 4M.
(2: 14) Sleepy Lagoon.

MARCH 1943.

Mutual Music Society Incorporated, 1270 6th Avenue, New York City, published "Glenn Miller's Method of Orchestral Arranging."

SECTION IV.

THE GLENN MILLER ARMY AIR FORCES ORCHESTRA, 1943 - 1945

(Known while in Europe as the American Band of the Allied Expeditionary Forces).

Note:—Due to the lack of information available, this section is grouped into two parts. The first part deals with the activities of the Orchestra before it left for England and has sections on the "I Sustain the Wings" broadcasts, V-Discs and AFRS Transcriptions, and the Victor Glenn Miller Army Air Force Band Album.

The second part deals with the Orchestra while in England and Europe and contains sections on AFRS Transcriptions and OWI discs, broadcast programmes, information about the Orchestra's sub-units, and various miscellaneous information.

OCTOBER 1942. Glenn Miller joins the United States Army as a Captain.

" I SUSTAIN THE WINGS" Radio programme broadcast from Yale University from July 1943 to June 1944.

17 JULY 1943—Yale University.

This was the first broadcast by the Orchestra which Capt. Glenn Miller had spent several months forming and moulding into shape.

Executive:

Director: Glenn Miller
Executive Officer: Don W. Haynes
Program Director: Paul Dudley
Production: George Voutsas; Harry Hartwick
Announcers: Paul Dubou; Broderick Crawford
Stage Manager: Julius Zifferblat

Personnel:—

TB Glenn Miller, Jimmy Priddy, Larry Hall, Jim Harwood, Dick Halliburton;
TP Zeke Zarchey, Steve Steck, Walter Holland, Jack Steele;
S Hank Freeman, Vince Carbone, Jack Saunderson, Jack Ferrier, Peanuts Hucko Clt.
Rh Louis Stein P; "Trigger" Alpert B; Carmen Mastren G; Ray McKinley D.
Vln 10 (Personnel Unknown)
Fr Horn—4 (Personnel Unknown)
a Glenn Miller, Jerry Gray, Mel Powell, Danny Gool, Perry Burgett.
VR Tony Martin, Bob Houston, Artie Malvin, Ray McKinley.
The Crew Chiefs (Steve Steck, Eugene Steck, Arthur Malvin, Murray Kane, Lynn Allison).

Personnel Changes:

When the Orchestra left for England on 22 June 1944 the personnel was as given on page 72.

AUGUST 1943—Bernie Priven TP joins the orchestra.

NOVEMBER 1943—Tony Martin VR; is replaced by Johnny Desmond.

MARCH 1944—Bob Carroll VR; joins the orchestra until it goes overseas.

Soon after the programme went on the air George Ockner joined as leader of the string section, a post which he held until the band broke up in 1945.

Air Checks—"I Sustain the Wings," broadcasts, mostly from the Vanderbilt Theater, New York.

The exact date of broadcast is unknown. Various vocal groups were heard—

The Glee Club (GC); The Quartet (4); The Crew Chiefs (CC); and the Ensemble (E).

(1: 32) Absent Minded. VR, JD.
(4: 19) Accentuate the Positive. VR, RM, CC.
(1: 00) Alexander's Rag Time Band.
(3: 18) Along the Santa Fe Trail. VR, JD.
(1: 20) All the Things You Are. VR, TM.
(1: 20) All Through The Night.
(1: 13) Alouette. VR, AM, GC.
(3: 11) American Patrol Int GM. American Patrol.
(1: 45) Amor. VR, JD.
(1: 33) Annie Laurie.
(3: 48) Anvil Chorus.
(2: 12) Army Air Corps Song. VR, TM, CC.
(3: 07) Army Air Corps Song. VR, JD, CC.
(3: 17) Army Air Corps Song. VR, JD, E.
(4: 04) Autumn Serenade. VR, JD
(3: 10) Begin the Beguine. VR, TM.
(3: 56) Begin the Beguine.
(1: 29) Birth of the Blues.
(1: 43) Blue Again.
(1: 40) Blue Champagne.
(1: 53) Blue Danube—Waltz.
(1: 56) Blue Hawaii.
(2: 00) Blue is the Night.
(1: 44) Blue Moon.
(1: 47) Blue Orchids. VR, JD.
(1: 49) Blue Orchids. VR, BC.
(1: 46) Blue Rain.
(2: 12) Blue Rain. Int GM.
(2: 33) Blue Rain. VR, JD.
(1: 12) Blue Room.
(1: 09) Blues Serenade.
(1: 24) Blue Skies.
(2: 38) Bombs Away. (Enlisted Man's Mess).
(1: 28) Brahms' Lullaby. VR, TM, GC.
(2: 07) Bye Bye Blues.
(1: 50) Caprice Viennois.
(2: 19) Caribbean Clipper.
(1: 41) Carry me back to Old Virginny.
(2: 31) Chattanooga Choo Choo. VR, RM, CC.
(2: 04) Cherokee.
(2: 20) Comin' in on a wing and a Prayer. VR, TM, E.
(1: 38) Deep Purple.
(2: 21) Dipsy Doodle.
(1: 40) Don't be that Way.
(0: 44) Do You Know. VR, JD.
(1: 26) Drink to me only with thine eyes.
(2: 52) Easter Parade. VR, JD, CC.
(1: 43) Eighteenth Century Drawing Room.
(2: 28) Enlisted Man's Mess (Bombs Away).
(1: 42) End of a perfect day.
(2: 42) Everybody Loves My Baby.
(2: 37) Farewell Blues.
(1: 39) Fellow on a Furlough. VR, JD.
(1: 29) Flow Gently Sweet Afton.
(2: 58) Flying Home
(1: 28) For the First Time.
(2: 26) Going Home.
(2: 51) G.I. Jive. VR, RM, CC.
(3: 32) Going My Way. VR, JD.
(2: 25) Goodnight wherever you are. VR, BC, CC.
(2: 19) Guns in the Sky. VR, JD, E.
(2: 01) Hallelujah.
(2: 37) Have you any gum, chum? VR, CC.
(2: 44) Here we go again.
(5: 43) Holiday for strings.
(2: 46) Hot time in the town of Berlin.
(3: 27) How Ya Gonna Keep 'Em Down On The Farm. VR, Carmen Mastren, CC, Band.
(2: 12) I can't give you anything but love, Baby. VR, "P." Hucko.
(1: 04) I couldn't sleep a wink, last night. VR, JD, CC.
(2: 20) I don't want to be loved. VR, JD.

(0: 46) If that's the way you want it, Baby. VR, CC; Int GM.
If you Please. VR, TM, CC.
(1: 48) If You Please. VR, TM, 4.
I hear ya screamin'.
(1: 32) I heard you cried last night. VR, TM.
(3: 14) I'll be around. VR, CC.
(1: 35) I'll be home for Christmas. VR, JD.
(1: 39) I Love You. VR, JD.
(3: 13) I never mention your name. VR, TM, 4.
(1: 59) In My Arms. VR, E.
(1: 51) In the Blue of Evening. VR, TM.
(1: 52) In the Blue of Evening. VR, JD.
(3: 05) In the Mood.
(2: 21) I only have eyes for you, dear. VR, JD.
(1: 40) Irresistible You. VR, JD, CC.
(1: 37) Irresistible You. VR, BC, CC.
(2: 41) It must be Jelly.
(3: 32) It's always You. VR, TM, 4.
(1: 29) It's Love, Love, Love. VR, CC
(3: 17) I've got a heart filled with love for you dear. VR, JD, CC.
(1: 12) I've got a heart filled with love for you dear. VR, BC, CC
(1: 16) I've got sixpence. VR, AM, E.
(1: 48) I want to be happy.
(1: 34) Jeannie with the light brown hair.
(2: 31) Jingle Bells. VR, LA, CC.
(1: 32) Johnny Zero. VR, AM, CC.
(1: 23) Killarney.
(1: 03) Later Tonight. VR, JD, CC.
(0: 42) Laura. VR, JD.
(2: 48) Little Brown Jug.
(1: 52) Loch Lomond.
(1: 35) Londonderry Air. (Danny Boy).
(3: 12) Long ago and far away. VR, JD.
(2: 05) Long ago and far away. VR, JD. (French and English lyrics).
(1: 23) Long Long Ago.
(2: 31) Lovely way to spend an evening. VR, JD, CC.
(1: 15) Make Believe.
(2: 03) Mighty Lak' a Rose.
(1: 18) Mister Luckie Me. VR, TM.
(2: 03) Mood Indigo.
(2: 34) Moon Dreams. VR, JD, CC.
(2: 30) Moonlight Serenade. (Concert Arr).
Moonlight Serenade.
(2: 10) Moonlight Sonata.
(1: 42) Mother Machree.
(1: 27) Music Makers.
(2: 00) Music Stopped. VR, JD.
(1: 29) My Blue Heaven.
(1: 52) My Buddy.
(2: 29) My Ideal. VR, JD.
(2: 00) My Isle of Golden Dreams.
(3: 04) Now I know. VR, JD.
(4: 12) Oh, what a beautiful morning. VR, JD, CC.
(1: 06) Old Black Joe.
(2: 16) Old Refrain.
(2: 20) On, Brave Old Army Team.
(2: 59) Outward Stomp.
(1: 41) Over There. VR, E.
(0: 50) Paper Doll. VR, CC.
(3: 35) Peggy the Pinup Girl. VR, RM, CC.
(2: 52) People will say we're in love. VR, TM.
(2: 22) Put your arms around me, me, honey. VR, TM, CC, E.
(4: 33) Pearls on Velvet.
(6: 07) Pistol Packin' Mama. VR, RM, CC.
(4: 31) Poinciana. VR, JD, CC.
(2: 03) Rhapsody in Blue. Int GM.
(2: 26) Saint Louis Blues.
(1: 41) Schubert's Serenade.
(2: 12) Serenade in Blue.
(1: 15) Shoo Shoo Baby. VR, CC.
(1: 02) Silent Night.
(1: 42) Silver Threads among the gold
(3: 08) Sleepy Town Train.
(1: 39) Smoke gets in your eyes.
(1: 02) Smoke Rings.
(1: 45) Snowfall.
(1: 27) Someone to love. VR, JD.
(1: 44) Songs my mother taught me.
(3: 53) Speak Low. VR, JD.
(3: 20) Stardust.
(1: 40) Star Eyes. VR, BC.
(4: 12) Stealing Apples.
(1: 27) Stompin' at the Savoy.
(3: 59) Stormy Weather.
(2: 35) Suddenly its Spring. VR, JD.
Suddenly its Spring. VR, JD. (French and English lyrics).
(1: 56) Summertime.
(0: 53) Sunday, Monday, or always. VR, TM.
(1: 31) Sweet and low.

(3: 24) Swing Low Sweet Chariot.
(3: 34) Swing Low Sweet Chariot. Tail End Charlie.
(1: 15) Take it easy. VR, CC, E.
(3: 26) There are the Yanks. VR, RM, CC.
(1: 31) Things ain't what they used to be.
(3: 22) Time alone will tell. VR, JD.
(2: 35) Time alone will tell. VR, BC.
(4: 10) Trolley Song. VR, JD, CC.
(3: 08) Tuxedo Junction.
(2: 44) Volga Boatmen.
(1: 34) Wabash Blues.
(1: 36) Wait for me Mary. VR, LA.
(2: 58) Wang Wang Blues.
(2: 07) Way you look tonight.
(2: 58) What do you do in the infantry. VR, CC.
(1: 43) White Christmas.
(2: 57) White Christmas. VR, JD.
(2: 05) Why Dream? VR, JD.
(2: 18) With my head in the clouds. VR, TM, 4, E; Int GM.
(1: 32) You'll never know. VR, TM.

Note:—There were many takes of many of these selections recorded from different programs, with different times, and sometimes different artists.

In late 1951 an American Collector had 21 of his private air checks of the "I Sustain the Wings" programs pressed in order to preserve them indefinitely. The cost of the two 10-in. LPs was very high so he had some extra copies pressed to defray the expense. The selections are different than those listed above. The two LP's are titled: "A Salute to Major Glenn Miller and His Army Air Force Orchestra."

Volume 1. Part 1. PR-101-A: 57-1.

(2: 00) My Blue Heaven. Int GM.
(2: 47) Goin' My Way. VR, JD.
(1: 37) It's Love, Love, Love. VR, CC
(3: 14) Long ago and far away. VR, JD.
(1: 00) Alexander's Rag Time Band.

Part 2. PR-101-B: 57-2.

(2: 00) Hallelujah.
(4: 00) Oh, what a beautiful morning. VR, JD, CC.
(1: 54) I'll be around. VR, JD, CC.
(1: 04) Stompin' at the Savoy.
(2: 15) Moon Dreams. VR, JD, CC.

Volume 2. Part 1. PR-102-A: 57-3.

(2: 00) Blues in My Heart.
(3: 05) Now I know. VR, JD.
(1: 25) Birth of the Blues.
(2: 41) Time alone will tell. VR, BC.
(3: 15) I got a heart filled with love for you, dear. VR, BC, CC.

Part 2. PR-102-B: 57-4.

(2: 12) Army Air Corps Song. VR, TM, CC.
(1: 00) I'm gonna buy a paper Doll. VR, CC.
(1: 44) All the things you are. VR, TM; Int, GM.
(1: 09) Blue Champagne.
(2: 00) In My Arms. VR, CC.
(2: 03) I Hear Ya Screamin'.

V-Discs

These were 12-in 78 rpm pressings produced exclusively for the Armed Forces Radio Service and for U.S. service centers, canteens and ships.

Many of the selections recorded were themselves air checks of "I Sustain the Wings" programs, while others were recorded by R.C.A. Victor especially for the Services.

All the V-Discs listed here are the "Army Series" (numbers below 515), or the "Combined Services Series" (numbers from 516 upwards), unless otherwise stated. Where selections are bracketed together they are on the same side of the disc.

JULY—DECEMBER 1943

CAPT. GLENN MILLER AND THE ARMY AIR FORCES TRAINING COMMAND ORCHESTRA

VP-264-D3-MC-286-1
(4: 15) **Stardust.** Int, GM. **V-D 65A**
VP-267-D3-MC-289-1

(4: 18) **Stormy Weather.** a JG. **V-D 91A.**

VP-415-D3-MC-481-1

(2: 29) **Squadron Song.** V, E.
(2: 35) **Tail End Charlie** } **V-D 144A.**

VP-416-D3-MC-482-1

(2: 05) **Going Home**
(1: 11) **Honeysuckle Rose.**
(1: 35) **My Blue Heaven.** } **V-D 123A,** Navy V-D 161B.

(3: 40) **Jersey Bounce.** V-D Unissued.

CAPT. GLENN MILLER & THE 418TH AAFTC BAND

VP-265-D3-MC-287-1

(2: 34) **Buckle down, Winsocki**—March
(1: 41) **El Capitan**—March } **V-D 91B**

VP-266-D3-MC-288-1

(4: 26) **St. Louis Blues March,** a JG. **V-D 65B,** N V-D 114A.

VP-1444-D5-TC-556-1

(4: 24) **St. Louis Blues.** a JG. **V-D 522A.**
(This is a second take of VP-266).

(4: 15) **Blues in the Night**—March. V-D Unissued.

JANUARY—MARCH 1944

CAPT. GLENN MILLER & THE AAFTC ORCHESTRA

VP-441-D4-TC-10-1

(1: 54) **Don't be that way.**
(1: 55) **Blue Champagne.** } **V-D 144B,** N V-D 160A.

VP-563-D4-TC-100-1

(1: 56) **Embraceable You**—Sgt. George Ockner and strings.
(2: 54) **G.I. Jive.** VR, RM, CC. } **V-D 183A.**

VP-618-D4-TC-125-1

(5: 10) **Moondreams.** VR, JD, CC. **V-D 201A,** N V-D 114B.

VP-655-D4-TC-157-1

(3: 21) **Stealing Apples.** **V-D 223B.** N V-D 3B
Special Services V-D 38B.

APRIL—JUNE 1944

CAPT. GLENN MILLER & THE AAFTC ORCHESTRA

VP-685-D4-TC-188-1

(3: 22) **I've got a heart filled with love for you, dear.** VR, JD, CC. **V-D 381A,** N V-D 161A.

VP-686-D4-TC-189-1

(2: 52) **Everybody loves my baby.** a JG.
(1: 13) **Stomping at the Savoy.** } **V-D 223A,** N V-D 3A
SS V-D 38A.

VP-687-D4-TC-190-1

(5: 03) **Poinciana.** a JG, VR, JD, CC. **V-D 242B,** N V-D 22B.

VP-702-D4-TC-197-1

(1: 59) **In the Gloaming.**
(1: 38) **Deep Purple.** } **V-D 302B,** N V-D 82B.

VP-703-D4-TC-198-1

(1: 41) **Fellow on a Furlough,** VR, JD.
(2: 13) **Guns in the Sky.** VR, JD, E. } **V-D 242A,** N V-D 22A.

VP-724-D4-TC-211-1

(2: 18) **Sun Valley Jump.** a JG.
(2: 35) **Chatanooga Choo Choo.** VR, RM, CC. } **V-D 281A,** N V-D 61A.

VP-725-D4-TC-212-1

(5: 37) **Holiday for Strings.** a JG. **V-D 421A,** N V-D 201A.

MAJOR GLENN MILLER & THE AAFTC ORCHESTRA

Note:—Although Glenn Miller did not have his promotion to Major at the time these discs were cut, by the time they were released he did have it. Some of the preceding series of cuts were reissued as by Major Glenn Miller.

VP-752-A
(1: 50) **My Buddy.** }
(2: 39) **Farewell Blues.** } **V-D 334A,** SS V-D 39A.

VP-1312-D5-TC-275-1
(1: 58) **Songs my Mother taught me.** }
(3: 00) **Peggy the Pinup Girl.** VR, RM, CC. } **V-D 533A.**

VP-1325-XP-34617-1
(1: 59) **Bye Bye Blues.** }
(2: 58) **Wang Wang Blues.** } **V-D 466A,** N V-D 246A.

VP-1330-XP-34644-1
(3: 07) **The Army Air Corps Song.** VR, JD, E }
(2: 00) **I hear you screaming.** } **V-D 504A.**

VP-1334-D5-TC-297-1
(2: 22) **I can't give you anything but love, baby.** VR, "P" Hucko. Int, PH. }
(2: 54) **Little Brown Jug.** } **V-D 482A.**

VP-1630-D5-TC-1495-1
(4: 01) **Symphony.** VR, JD. **V-D 601A,** SS V-D 41A.

VP-1632-D5-TC-1542-1
(2: 00) **Why Dream.** VR, JD. }
(2: 57) **Passage Interdit.** } **V-D 587A.**

J-560-ND7-TC-1464-1
(2: 35) **In the Mood.** (Labelled as "Glenn Miller's Overseas Orchestra"). Bert Hirst V-Disc Orch. } **V-D 842 A.**

Note:—It is thought that some of the later Miller AAFTC V-Discs listed above may have been recorded by the Band in England, and the masters sent back to the States for processing and issue.

The following record is labelled "Seventeen Skymen of the 718th AAF Band." It is reputed to be a Glenn Miller disc, and sounds not unlike the Miller AAFTC Orchestra.

VP-962-D4-TC-464-1
(4: 55) **Summer Holiday.** **V-D 338B.**

The following sides by the Miller civilian band are taken from Victor masters. They are included here to clear up any confusion. The Victor master number is given in brackets.

VP-
Moonlight Mood. (074737) **V-D 12B.**

VP-64-D3-MC-127-1
Sleepy Town Train (074747) **V-D 201B.**

VP-75-D3-MC-138-1
Moonlight Serenade. (035701) **V-D 39A,** N V-D 160B.

VP-139-D3-MC-3368-1
At Last. (072285) **V-D 12A.**

VP-159-D3-MC-190-1
My Melancholy Baby (046736) **V-D 39B.**

VP-333-D3-MC-423-1

In the Mood (038171) **V-D 123B.**

VP-977-D3-MC-475-1

Missouri Waltz. (046432) } **V-D 352B.**
Alice Blue Gown. (048485) }

Note:—V-Discs were not released after 15 June 1949. When the Korean War broke out in July 1950, a new series of records was started, and called "Armed Forces Records." These were similar to V-Discs in all respects except that they do not have issue numbers. There is just a code number for each side.

There are two known Miller civilian selections on these discs.

10-30	**AFR-50**	BENNY GOODMAN **Adios**	(064474)
10-62	**AFR-112**	**Jingle Bells**	(071192)

AFRS TRANSCRIPTIONS

P-16	Pt. 1	(17-1768)	**Bubble bath / Blue Danube Waltz / Blue is the Night / Everybody loves my baby.**
	Pt. 2	(17-1769)	**Seven-o-five / Along the Sante Fe Trail / Farewell Blues / Hot time in the town of Berlin.**
P-		(17-1822)	**Theme / Caribbean Clipper / Time alone will tell / Jeannie with the light brown hair / With my head in the Clouds.**
P-101		(SSL—137)	**Moonlight Serenade / Rhapsody in Blue / Little Brown Jug / Peggy the Pin-up Girl.**
P-106		(SSL—146)	**Moon Dreams / Eighteenth Century Drawing Room / Farewell Blues / Don't be that way / Blue Champagne.**
P-121		( )	**Stompin' at the Savoy / Homesick / Tail End Charlie / Feeling in the moonlight / American Patrol / Pagan Love Song.**
P-292		(SSL—582)	**Put your arms around me honey / Dipsy Doodle / Sun Valley Jump / In the Mood.**
P-293		(SSL—583)	**String of Pearls / Cherokee / American Patrol / Anvil Chorus.**
P-297		(SSL—613)	**Volga Boatmen / Annie Laurie / I hear ya Screamin' / Snafu Jump.**
P-298		(SSL—614)	**What do you do in the infantry / Juke Box Saturday Night / There are the Yanks / Jeep Jockey Jump.**
P-299		(SSL—615)	**Over There / Mission to Moscow / It must be Jelly / Enlisted Men's Mess.**
P-300		(SSL—616)	**Sleepy Town Train / Speak Low / Now I know.**

MARINE CORPS AFRS TRANSCRIPTIONS

Pro-230	Pt. 1	**Head in the clouds / Mission to Moscow / Over There.**
	Pt. 2	**Dipsy Doodle / In the Mood / Put your arms around me.**
Pro-292	Pt. 1	**Enlisted Men's Mess / It must be Jelly / Sleepy Town Train / Speak Low.**
	Pt. 2	**Holiday for Strings / Now I know / What a Beautiful Morning.**

TREASURY STAR PARADE TRANSCRIPTIONS

Pro-309	(G-6685)	**Moonlight Serenade / American Patrol / How Sweet you are / Juke Box Saturday Night.**
Pro-314	(G-6686)	**Moonlight Serenade / In the Mood / My heart tells me / Holiday for strings / Victory Polka.**
Pro-380		Miller background music for play "Combat Crew".

MUSICA DE LAS FUERZAS AERAS

Prog 1.	(ND4MM 5233)	**I hear ya screamin' / My heart tells me / String of Pearls / Put your arms around me, Honey.**

OVERSEAS BRANCH—OFFICE OF WAR INFORMATION TRANSCRIPTIONS

Outpost Concert Series No. 12—Music of the Jazz (*sic*) Bands:—

No. 24—Capt. Glenn Miller and his AAFTC Band.

	( )	**Holiday for strings** (*strings only*) / **Hallelujah (Tail end Charlie) / Oh what a beautiful Morning.** VR, JD / **Whaddya do in the Infantry.**

No. 23—A Program of Boogie Woogie.

Music from America—Unannounced Popular Series:—

Prog. No. 11	(ND4-MM-5988) (17-1621)	**Flying Home / Moonlight Serenade** (*full version*) / **String of Pearls / Guns in the sky.**
Prog. No. 12	(ND4-MM-5989) (17-1617)	**I hear you screaming / How sweet you are / Going Home / Little Brown Jug.**
Prog. No. 17	(17-1805)	**9.20 Special / Going my way.** VR, JD / **Just the way you look tonight / Lady be Good.**
Prog No. 18	(17-1808)	**Long tall mama / Our Waltz** (*strings only*) / **My Blue Heaven / Swing low sweet chariot.**
Prog. No. 20 (*single-sided disc*)	(17-1819)	**Here we go again / Annie Laurie** (*strings only*) / **Goodnight wherever you are.** VR, JD / **Music Makers.**
Prog. No. 21	(17-1817)	**Tuxedo Junction / Fellow on a Furlough.** VR, JD / **Summertime / I've got a heart filled with love.**
Prog. No. 23	(17-1872)	**Mission to Moscow / Irresistable you.** VR, JD / **Going Home / There'll be hot time in the town of Berlin.**

The Glenn Miller Army Air Force Band Album

In September 1955 R.C.A. Victor produced the first commercially issued recordings by Capt. Glenn Miller and the A.A.F. Orchestra (the only previous public release of records by the A.A.F. Orchestra had been the "bootleg" A.F.N. LP's (see page 77) which were supressed by legal action in 1954).

The Victor recordings consisted of five 12-inch LP's in a special Album similar in format to the two civilian Miller Band Limited Editions. The Album also contained descriptive notes by George T. Simon, many excellent photos of the A.A.F. Orchestra (mostly pictures taken in England), a list of personnel and a full list of selections with vocal and instrumental solo credits for each tune. Most of the items were extracts from "I Sustain the Wings" radio broadcasts by the Orchestra in the United States—no exact broadcast dates were given in the Album but they would all date presumably from the period July 17, 1943, to about June 21, 1944.

The recordings were also issued in Extended Play form in an Album. The E.P. number is given in brackets in the listing below.

In view of the make-up of the Album and in the interests of conserving space in this Discography this Album is listed fully below only and not in Section V as well as are the other commercial L.P.'s.—*G.E.B.*

"GLENN MILLER ARMY AIR FORCE BAND". Victor LPT6702.
10-12-in. sides (Victor EPOT6702, 30-7-in. sides)

Side	*Master*	*Title, etc.*	*Label No.*
1.	**F2PP-4748**	**Over there.** VR, E. **A lovely way to spend an Evening.** VR, JD, CC. **The G.I. Jive.** VR, RM, CC. Medley: **Flow gently, Sweet Afton.** **Moondreams.** VR, JD, CC. **Don't be that way.** **Blue Champagne.** **Holiday for strings.**	**LPT-6702-1**
2.	**F2PP-4749**	**Peggy the Pin-up Girl.** VR, RM, CC. **Going my way.** VR, JD. Medley: **I dream of Jeanie.** **I couldn't sleep a wink last night.** VR, JD, CC. **Alexander's Ragtime Band.** **Blue Rain.** **I've got a heart filled with love.** VR, JD. AM, CC. **Anvil Chorus.**	**LPT-6702-2**
3.	**F2PP-4750**	**There are Yanks.** VR, JD, RM, CC. **Stardust.** **Song of the Volga Boatmen.** **How sweet you are.** VR, JD. **Pearls on Velvet.** Ftg Mel Powell P. **There'll be a hot time in the town of Berlin.** VR, RM, CC.	**LPT-6702-3**
4.	**F2PP-4751**	**What do you do in the Infantry.** VR, AM, CC. **Farewell Blues.** **Sun Valley Jump.** Medley: **In the Gloaming.** **For the first time.** VR, JD. **Stomping at the Savoy.** **Deep Purple.** **Stormy Weather.**	**LPT-6702-4**
5.	**F2PP-4752**	**Mission to Moscow.** **My Ideal.** VR, JD. **Tuxedo Junction.** **In an 18th Century Drawing Room.** **I hear you screaming.** **I'll be around.** VR, JD, CC. **Poinciana.**	**LPT-6702-5**

Side	*Master*	*Title, etc.*	*Label No.*
6.	**F2PP-4753**	**Flying Home.** **Long ago and far away.** VR, JD. **It must be Jelly.** Medley: **Going Home** **Goodnight wherever you are.** VR, JD, CC. **I can't give you anything but love.** **Wang Wang Blues.** **Here we go again.**	**LPT-6702-5**
7.	**F2PP-4754**	**Jeep Jockey Jump.** **Blues in my heart.** **Juke-box Saturday night.** VR, CC, AM. **People will say we're in love.** VR, JD. **St. Louis Blues March.** **Time alone will tell.** VR, BC. **Victory Polka.** VR, JD, CC, E.	**LPT-6702-4**
8.	**F2PP-4755**	**Air Corps Song.** VR, E. **Suddenly it's Spring.** VR, JD. **I love you.** VR, JD. Medley: **Long long ago.** **The music stopped.** VR, JD. **The Dipsey Doodle.** **Wabash Blues.** **Everybody loves my baby.**	**LPT-6702-3**
9.	**F2PP-4756**	**Enlisted men's mess.** **Absent Minded.** VR, JD. **My Blue Heaven.** **I got sixpence.** VR, AM. **Begin the Beguine.** **Blue is the night.** **In the Mood.** **Oh, what a beautiful morning.** VR, JD, CC.	**LPT-6702-2**
10.	**F2PP-4757**	**Tail-End Charlie.** **Speak Low.** VR, JD. Medley: **Londonderry Air.** **Shoo Shoo Baby.** VR, CC, AM. **The way you look tonight.** **Blue Danube.** **Pistol-packing Mama.** VR, Carmen Mastren, RM, CC.	**LPT-6702-1**

Note:—On June 29, 1944, the Miller organization landed in England. An official U.S. Signal Corps photograph dated 30 September, 1944, shows the following personnel:—

Executive:

Director:	Major Glenn Miller.
Executive Officer:	Lieutenant Don W. Haynes.
Program Director:	Warrant Officer Paul Dudley.
Production:	T/Sgt. George Voutsas; Sgt. Harry Hartwick.
Announcers:	Cpl. Paul Dubou, Sgt. Broderick Crawford.
Stage Manager:	Sgt. Julius Zifferblat.

Personnel:

TB Major Glenn Miller, Sgt. Jimmy Priddy, Cpl. John Halliburton, Cpl. Larry Hall, PFC Nat Peck;
TP M/Sgt. Zeke Zarchey, Sgt. Bobby Nichols, Sgt. Whitey Thomas, Sgt. Bernie Priven, Cpl. Jack Steele;
S S/Sgt. Hank Freeman, Sgt. Vince Carbone, Cpl. Mannie Thaler, Cpl. Fred Guerra, Cpl. Jack Ferrier, Sgt. Michael "Peanuts" Hucko, Clt & TS;
Rh Sgt. Mel Powell P; Sgt. "Trigger" Alpert B; Sgt. Carmen Mastren G; Sgt. Ray Mckinley D;

Fr. Horn Cpl. Addison Collins;
Vln S/Sgt. George Ockner—Leader and Concert Master;
S/Sgt. Harry Katzman—Assistant Leader;
S/Sgt. Carl Swanson, Sgt. Dave Herman, Sgt. Dave Schwartz, Cpl. Eugene Bergen, Cpl. Morris Bailkin, Cpl. Henry Brynan, Cpl. Earl Cornwell, Cpl. Phil. Cogliano, Cpl. Milton Edelson, Cpl. Stanley Harris, Cpl. Nat Kaproff, Cpl. Ernest Kardos, Cpl. Joseph Kowalewski, Cpl. Richard Motolinski, Cpl. Bob Ripley, Cpl. David Sackson, Cpl. Emmanuel Wishnow, PFC Fred Ostrovsky;
Vla Cpl. Stanley Hank;
a T/Sgt. Jerry Gray, M/Sgt. Norman Leyden, S/Sgt. Ralph Wilkinson, S/Sgt. Jimmy Jackson;
Some by: Major Glenn Miller, Sgt. Mel Powell, Sgt. Carmen Mastren;
VR Sgt. Johnny Desmond, Sgt. Ray McKinley, the Crew Chiefs. (Crew Chiefs—Sgt. Steve Ste ck, Cpl. Eugene Steck, Cpl. Arthur Malvin Cpl. Murray Kane, Cpl. Lynn Allison);

Reliefs: Sgt. Steve Steck TP; Jack Saunderson S; Joe Schulman B; Al Milton G; Cpl. Jack Russin P; Cpl. Frank Ippolito D.

Note:—The Miller organisation was stationed first in Chelsea, S.W. London; then after a few days they moved to Bedford where they were based until they went to France in December 1944. Their general assignment was to broadcast over the newly-opened Allied Expeditionary Forces Programme of the B.B.C. to the troops fighting on the Continent, and to do live shows for forces stationed in the United Kingdom. They broadcast mostly from the Corn Exchange in Bedford and, later, from the Queensbury All-Services Club (actually the Casino Theatre) in Soho, London.—*G.E.B.*

B.B.C. BROADCASTS.

The following broadcast schedule operated from 12 November, 1944; some earlier programmes are listed below (pp. 74-78).—*G.E.B.*

"The American Band of the A.E.F."—Tuesday and Friday evenings, 8.30, 30 mins.

"The American Dance Band" (The Swing Shift), directed by Sgt. Ray McKinley (The Orchestra minus the strings)—30 mins, twice a week, evenings.

"The Strings with Wings," directed by Sgt. George Ockner—15 mins, twice a week, usually Monday and Wednesday evenings.

"The Swing Sextet" (the "Uptown Hall"), led by Sgt. Mel Powell—15 mins, three times a week, evenings.

"A Soldier and a Song," Sgt Johnny Desmond accompanied by the full A.E.F. Orchestra—10 or 15 mins, three times a week, evenings.

"Piano Parade" by Cpl. Jack Russin—15 minutes, three mornings a week.

Most of these programmes were repeated (recorded) during the next morning or afternoon. In addition, the Orchestra, and various parts of it, took part in various other programmes as guests.

They also broadcast over the American Forces Network, then operating in the United Kingdom.

Many of the broadcasts by the full Orchestra were also heard on the B.B.C. Home Service, sometimes as recordings.

9 JULY 1944—(A.F.N.) "HEADQUARTERS BAND, U.S. ARMY"

Compere: Leslie Mitchell; *guest stars*: Dorothy Carless and Bruce Trent.

Moonlight Serenade / March of the Torch of Liberty / In the Mood / Stardust / Begin the Beguine. VR, DC / Flying Home / Medley: My Buddy; Now I Know. VR, JD; Music Makers; Farewell Blues / G.I. Jive. VR, RM & E / I Couldn't Sleep a Wink Last Night. VR, BT / Poinciana / What Do We Do in the Infantry?

13 JULY 1944—Home Service AMERICAN BAND OF THE SUPREME ALLIED COMMAND.

Compere: Capt. Miller (introduced by Jean Metcalf); *guest stars* DC & BT. *Note:*—Capt. Miller usually compered, unless otherwise stated.

American Patrol / Summertime / Juke Box Saturday Night. VR, CC / I couldn't sleep a wink last night. VR, DC / It must be Jelly / Without a Song. VR, BT / Holiday For Strings.

20 JULY 1944—Home Service AMERICAN BAND OF THE SUPREME ALLIED COMMAND

Guest stars: Vera Lynn, Sgt. Jimmy Miller, R.A.F.

Caribbean Clipper / This is a lovely way to spend an evening. VR, JM / Put your arms around me honey. VR, JD & E / Medley: Mighty like a Rose; Amor, Amor. VR, JD; Chatanooga Choo Choo; Bye Bye Blues / Besame Moucho. VR, VL / The Anvil Chorus.

Note:—It is not known exactly when the Orchestra assumed the title "American Band of the A.E.F."–these early programmes were announced as shown above.—*G.E.B.*

27 JULY 1944—London

The whole Miller A.E.F. Orchestra and singers played a special half-hour stage show at the charity premiere at the Plaza Cinema of the Bing Crosby film "Going My Way". This was one of the only two public appearances by the Orchestra in London. — *G.E.B.*

In the Mood / Juke Box Saturday Night. VR, CC / Holiday for Strings / Poinciana. VR, JD & CC / The G.I. Jive. VR, RM / The Anvil Chorus.

27 JULY 1944 AMERICAN BAND OF THE SUPREME ALLIED COMMAND.

(Broadcast was probably from the Paris Cinema (B.B.C. studio), W.1)
Guest star: Anne Shelton.

Flying Home / Smoke gets in your Eyes / The Victory Polka. VR, CC & Ensemble / I'll Get By. VR, AS / Medley: In the Gloamin'; Fellow on a Furlough. VR, JD; Stomping at the Savoy; Deep Purple / Time alone will tell. VR, JD / Song of the Volga Boatmen.

3 August 1944 AMERICAN BAND OF THE SUPREME ALLIED COMMAND.

Guest Stars: Dinah Shore, Sam Browne.

Sun Valley Jump / Time on My Hands. VR, SB / Must be Jelly / Long ago and far away. VR, DS / Medley: Flow Gently, Sweet Afton; Moondreams. VR, JD; Don't be that way; Blue Champagne / I'll be seeing you. VR, DS / With my head in the clouds. VR, CC & E.

6 August 1944—The Miller A.E.F. Band were among the guest stars in "Variety Bandbox" broadcast—they played the following numbers:

Moonlight Serenade / In the Mood / Stardust / Poinciana / American Patrol / Time alone will tell. VR, JD / Holiday for Strings.

10 August 1944 AMERICAN BAND OF THE SUPREME ALLIED COMMAND.

Guest star: Paula Green.

Tail End Charlie / Body and Soul / Tessa's Torch Song. VR, PG / Medley: Danny Boy; All My Life. VR, JD; Cherokee; Blue Danube / Holiday for Strings.

On this date Capt. Glenn Miller was promoted Major.

17 August 1944—A.E.F. Prog. AMERICAN BAND OF THE SUPREME ALLIED COMMAND.

Guest star: Beryl Davis.

I Hear You Screaming / Stormy Weather / It's Love, Love, Love. VR, BD / Medley: Mother Macree; I couldn't sleep a wink last night. VR, JD; I can't give you anything but love, baby; The Wang Wang Blues / Pearls on Velvet / The Casson Song.

24 August 1944 AMERICAN BAND OF THE SUPREME ALLIED COMMAND

Guest star: Doreen Villiers.

Swing Low, Sweet Chariot / I'll be seeing you. VR, JD / That's Sabotage. VR, DV / Medley: Long Ago; The Music Stopped. VR, JD; Dipsy Doodle; Blues in my heart / I'm heading for California. VR, RM, CC / American Patrol.

1 September 1944 AMERICAN BAND OF THE SUPREME ALLIED COMMAND

Guest star: Bing Crosby. (*Note*—Bing sang on about half a dozen programmes with the full Orchestra and various sub-units at this time).

Here we go again / Long Ago and Far Away. VR, BC / Medley: My Buddy; Amor, Amor. VR, BC; Music Makers; Farewell Blues / Swinging on a Star. VR, BC / Poinciana. VR, BC.

3 September 1944 A SOLDIER AND A SONG.

Bing Crosby replaced Sgt. Johnny Desmond on this occasion.

Amor, Amor / Long Ago and Far Away / White Christmas / I'll be seeing you (all Crosby vocals—needless to say!)

7 SEPTEMBER 1944 — AMERICAN BAND OF THE SUPREME ALLIED COMMAND

Guest star: Gloria Brent.

In the Mood / Body and Soul / Tuxedo Junction / Medley: Songs my Mother taught me; It's Love, Love, Love. VR, CC; In an Eighteenth-Century Drawing Room; Blue Orchids. VR, JD / Time alone will tell. VR, GB / All's well, Mademoiselle. a Jerry Gray.

10 SEPTEMBER 1944 — A SOLDIER AND A SONG

Time On My Hands (*theme*) / My Heart Stood Still / It Could Happen To You / Breaking In A New Pair Of Shoes (*Orch.*) / I'll be Seeing You.

14 SEPTEMBER 1944 — AMERICAN BAND OF THE SUPREME ALLIED COMMAND

Guest star: Paula Green.

Get Happy / At Last. VR, PG / I've got a heart filled with love. VR, JD / Medley: Schubert's Serenade; Irresistable You. VR, JD & CC; Little Brown Jug; Rhapsody in Blue / Parachute Jump (*Quartet*: Hucko, Powell, Alpert, McKinley) / The Victory Polka. VR, JD, CC, Ensemble.

16 SEPTEMBER 1944—London.

The Miller A.E.F. Orchestra and Dinah Shore took part in a recording session at the HMV studios. The recordings were for the U.S. authorities and were never issued commercially.—*G.E.B.*

Stardust. VR DS.
All I Do Is Dream Of You. VR, DS.
I've Got A Heart Filled With Love For You, Dear. VR, JD, CC.
Farewell Blues. (*Orchestra*)

17 SEPTEMBER 1944 — A SOLDIER AND A SONG

Time On My hands (*theme*) / Where or When / Here we go again (*Orchestra*) / Without a Song.

21 SEPTEMBER 1944 — AMERICAN BAND OF THE SUPREME ALLIED COMMAND

Guest stars: Mus. i/c Sam Donohue and the U.S. Navy Band.

Flying Home / I'll Be Seeing You. VR, JD / Somebody Loves Me (*Navy Band*) / Medley: Jeannie with the Light Brown Hair; I couldn't sleep a wink last night. VR, JD & CC; Begin the Beguine; Blue Rain / L.S.T. Party (*Navy Band*) / One O'Clock Jump (*combined Miller and Navy Bands*).

28 SEPTEMBER 1944 — AMERICAN BAND OF THE A.E.F.

Guest star: Pat Kirkwood.

Get Happy / Long Ago and Far Away. VR, JD / Is you is or is you ain't my baby? VR, RM / Medley: Flow gently, Sweet Afton; Moondreams. VR, JD; Don't be that way; Blue Champagne / My Kind of Music. VR, PK / Anvil Chorus.

5 OCTOBER 1944 — AMERICAN BAND OF THE A.E.F.

Guest star: R.S.M. George Melachrino (conductor of the British Band of the A.E.F.)

Great Day / Goodnight, Good Neighbour. VR, GMel / String of Pearls / Medley: Caprice Viennoise; I'll walk Alone. VR, JD; My Isle of Golden Dreams; Birth of the Blues / It could happen to You. VR, JD / What do we do in the Infantry.

12 October 1944 AMERICAN BAND OF THE A.E.F.

Guest star: Jack Hylton.

Caribbean Clipper / My Prayer. VR, JD / Mission to Moscow / Medley: Going Home; Star Eyes. VR, JD; Honeysuckle Rose; My Blue Heaven / She shall have Music (*Orchestra conducted by* Jack Hylton) / Poinciana. VR, JD, CC.

15 October 1944—London.

The whole Miller A.E.F. Orchestra and singers appeared at the Jazz Jamboree charity concert at the Stoll Theatre, Kingsway. This was the Orchestra's second and last public appearance in London. During the Miller spot, Victor Feldman (then a "boy wonder" drummer, aged about seven) played a number, "Sweet Georgia Brown," with a quartet from the Orchestra. The Miller programme included In the Mood / Juke Box Saturday Night / Holiday for Strings, Song of the Volga Boatmen; Sgt. Johnny Desmond sang.—*G.E.B.*

21 October 1944—Gen. Forces Prog.—

AMERICAN BAND OF THE A.E.F.

26 October 1944 AMERICAN BAND OF THE A.E.F.

Guest star: Anne Shelton.

American Patrol / Stardust / On, Wisconsin / Medley: Old Refrain; Same old Love. VR, JD; Smoke gets in your eyes; Blue Again / Spring will be a little late this year. VR, AS / You are my sunshine. VR, JD, CC.

1 November 1944—England.

Major Glenn Miller and the "American Band of the Supreme Allied Command" began a series of half hour broadcasts every Wednesday from 1330 to 1400 (1: 30 - 2: 00 p.m.) on the German "Wermacht Hour." They were aired from the American Broadcasting Station in Europe. The programs were probably recorded as transcriptions. The first program featured the following selections: "In the Mood," "Star Dust," "Song of the Volga Boatmen," "Is you is, or is you ain't my baby?", "Great Day," and "Moonlight Serenade."

In February 1952 two illegal LP's appeared on the record market in New York. These two LP's were labelled "An AFN Presentation—Major Glenn Miller and the AEF Orchestra." There were two volumes. They were very poorly recorded and were supressed by the Glenn Miller Estate.

The majority of the selections on the disks were dubbed from poor air checks of propaganda broadcasts beamed at Germany in late 1944. The announcements are made in German and English by Major Glenn Miller, and a German refugee identified only as "Ilsa."

Volume 1—Part 1 of "An AFN Presentation"

(0: 15) **Introduction** by Ilsa.
(0: 47) **Moonlight Serenade.** Int GM, Ilsa.
(4: 11) **American Patrol.** Int GM, Ilsa.
(4: 32) **Great Day.** Int Ilsa.
(4: 04) **String of Pearls.** Int GM, Ilsa.

Part 2 of "An AFN Presentation"

(3: 33) **In the Mood.**
(4: 59) **Poinciana.** VR, Artie Melvin, CC.
(4: 04) **Now I Know.** VR, JD (German lyrics); Int GM, JD, Ilsa.

Volume II—Part 1 of "An AFN Presentation"

(2: 49) **Begin the Beguine.**
(2: 42) **Summertime.** Int GM, Ilsa.
(3: 40) **Song of the Volga Boatmen.** Int GM, Ilsa.
(3: 49) **My Heart Tells Me.** VR, JD (German lyrics); Int GM, Ilsa.

Part 2 of "An AFN Presentation."

(3: 43) **Tuxedo Junction.** Int GM, Ilsa.
(3: 52) **Is you is or is you ain't my baby.** VR, RM; Int GM, JD, RM, Ilsa.
(3: 50) **Anvil Chorus.** Int GM, Ilsa.
(0: 43) **Moonlight Serenade.** Farewell announcement by GM, Ilsa.

2 November 1944 AMERICAN BAND OF THE A.E.F.

No guest stars from now on.

Get Happy / I'll be seeing You. VR, JD / Anchors Aweigh / Medley: Long, Long Ago; The Music Stopped. VR, JD; Dipsy Doodle; Blues in my heart / Have you got any Gum, Chum? VR, JD, CC / Jerry's Aachen Back (*Quartet;* Hucko, Powell, Alpert, McKinley) / Song of the Volga Boatmen.

6 November 1944

Sir Adrian Boult conducted the Strings with Wings. Programme included "Serenade for Strings" (Elgar), "Clouds" Nocturne (Debussy), "Maid with the Flaxen Hair" (Debussy).

9 November 1944 AMERICAN BAND OF THE AEF.

Jeep Jockey Jump / It could happen to You; VR, JD / On, Brave Old Army Team / Medley: Londonderry Air; Spring will be a little late this year; Cherokee; Blue Danube / Is you is or is you ain't my baby? VR, RM / Flying Home.

Note:—Miller announced that the Orchestra will be on the air every Tuesday and Friday from next week. (All the above listed A.E.F. programmes were on Thursday evenings at 8.30 p.m.). (*See also* Note on page 73)—*G.E.B.*

14 November 1944 AMERICAN BAND OF THE A.E.F. (*cond.* J. Gray).

Compere: Sgt. Keith Jameson.

Here we go again / Body and Soul / Beat me Daddy eight to a Bar. VR, RM / Medley: My Buddy; Now I Know. VR, JD; Music Makers; Farewell Blues, Deep Summer Music. VR, JD / I hear you Screaming.

17 November 1944 AMERICAN BAND OF THE A.E.F. (*cond.* J. Gray).

Compere: Sgt. Keith Jameson.

Seven-o-five / Sweet Lorraine. VR, Artie Melvin / Tuxedo Junction / Medley: Jeannie with the light brown hair; Amor, Amor. VR, AM; Begin the Beguine; Blue Rain / Down the Road A-piece. VR, RM / Great Day.

21 November 1944 AMERICAN BAND OF THE A.E.F. (*cond* GM again)

Tail-end Charlie / Rhapsody in Blue / The G.I. Jive. VR, RM / Medley: Mother Macree; It could happen to you. VR, Artie Melvin; I can't give you anything but love; Wang Wang Blues / Little Brown Jug / You are My Sunshine. VR, JD, CC.

23 NOVEMBER 1944 THE SWING SHIFT.

Anchors Aweigh / Rhapsody in Blue / Got any Gum Chum? VR, AM, CC / I Dream of You. VR, AM / Pass Over Lightly (*trio;* Hucko, Powell, McKinley) / Now I Know. VR, AM / On Army Team.

24 NOVEMBER 1944 AMERICAN BAND OF THE A.E.F.

Long Ago and Far Away. VR, AM / Mission to Moscow / Medley: Mighty like a Rose; Amor, Amor. VR; AM; Chatanooga Choo Choo. VR, RM, CC; Bye Bye Blues / String of Pearls / Oranges and Lemons. a Jerry Gray. VR, AM, CC.

28 NOVEMBER 1944 AMERICAN BAND OF THE A.E.F.

In the Mood / Sweet and Lovely. VR, JD / Juke Box Saturday Night. VR, CC. / Medley: Flow gently, Sweet Afton; Moondreams. VR, JD, CC; Don't be that way; Blue Champagne / Everybody loves my baby / Poinciana.

31 NOVEMBER 1944 AMERICAN BAND OF THE A.E.F.

Great Day / White Christmas. VR, JD / Swing low Sweet Chariot / Medley: All through the Night; Time waits for no-one. VR, JD; Take it Easy; Blue Hawaii / Tea for Two (*Quartet* Hucko, Powell, Alpert, McKinley) / Holiday for Strings.

5 DECEMBER 1944 AMERICAN BAND OF THE A.E.F.

Guest star: Morton Downey.

Everybody loves my baby / It had to be you. VR, JD / Medley: Long, long ago; The Music Stopped; The Dipsy Doodle; Blues in My Heart / I'll Get By. VR, MD / The Red Cavalry March / Stomping at the Savoy (*instead of usual theme*).

SEPTEMBER - DECEMBER 1944—London.

OVERSEAS WAR INFORMATION / OFFICE OF WAR INFORMATION DISCS.

These were part of the "General Stockpile Transcriptions." They are believed to have been recorded in England. Many of the selections were issued on the OWI-Discs which were similar to V-Discs, being 12-in. 78 r.p.m. discs issued for the US Forces.

13-4295		**Little Brown Jug.**	
13-4362		**Mission to Moscow.**	
13-4363	(3: 00)	**Jeep Jockey Jump.**	DM-1 MF-1964
13-4364		**Tuxedo Junction.**	
13-4397		**Song of the Volga Boatmen.**	
13-4484	(3: 08)	**In the Mood.**	DM-3 MF-2214
13-4485	(2: 36)	**Sun Valley Jump.**	DM-3 MF-2211
13-4486	(2: 00)	**Cherokee.**	DM-4 MF-2211
13-4487	(4: 01)	**Here we go again.**	DM-3 MF-2211
13-4573	(3: 08)	**9.20 Special.**	DM-4 MF-2411
13-4574	(3: 00)	**Oh Lady be Good.**	
13-4575	(3: 26)	**Bubble Bath.**	DM-4 MF-2411
13-4576	(2: 54)	**Everybody loves my Baby.**	MF-2411
13-4733	(3: 17)	**Begin the Beguine.**	DM-7 MF-2413
13-4735	(2: 55)	**Snafu Jump.**	MF-2413
13-4437	(3: 09)	**Tail end Charlie.**	DM-7 MF-2413
OSA-5	(2: 38)	**Enlisted Men's Mess.**	
OSA-6	(2: 29)	**I hear ya Screamin.'**	MF-2163
OSA-7	(1: 38)	**Don't be that way.**	
OSA-8	(3: 25)	**String of Pearls.**	

AFRS TRANSCRIPTIONS—These were probably recorded in England.

P-501 (SSL-1015) **Tuxedo Junction / Symphony / Rhapsody in Blue / In the Middle of May.**
P-502 (SSL-1016) **Passai en a dit / Homesick / Swing low Sweet Chariot / The More I See You.**
P-517 (SSL-1045) **Things ain't what they used to be / Poinciana / Why Dream / Seven O Five.**
P-602 (SSL-1198) **Here we go again / American Patrol / Oranges and Lemons.**
P-604 (SSL-1200) **Blue is the Night / I can't give you anything but love / I don't want to be loved / Tail end Charlie.**
P-701 ( ) **Anvil Chorus / Things ain't what they used to be / Mission to Moscow / Cherokee.**
GT-101 **Homesick / Passage Interdit / Star Dust.**

About the end of November, orders came from SHAEF for the Orchestra to proceed to France: Miller had wanted to play to the troops as near to the actual fighting as possible. In two weeks, the Orchestra and its various sub-units pre-recorded 129 programmes for use by the B.B.C. after the Miller men had gone to France, and in this time they played all their usual live broadcasts as well! Air transport to the Continent was arranged and they prepared to leave Bedford.

15 December 1944.

Major Glenn Miller and two other officers took off in a USAAF plane from an airfield near Bedford in poor flying conditions.

18 December 1944.

The Orchestra flew to Paris, to find no word of Major Miller's arrival there. Intensive searching failed to locate either his plane or any of its passengers.

24 December 1944

SHAEF announced that Major Glenn Miller had been posted "missing."

25 December 1944—Paris.

The American Band of the A.E.F., conducted by Sgt Jerry Gray, broadcast from the Olympia Theatre in the B.B.C.'s "A.E.F. Christmas Show."

After Major Miller disappeared, the Orchestra continued its concerts and broadcasts—conducted by Sgt. Jerry Gray on the air, and by Sgt. Ray McKinley at stage shows. The programmes by the full Orchestra were now announced by Warrant Officer Paul Dudley (programme director). Later, they toured France, Belgium, Holland and Germany playing to Allied forces.

The following is a listing of a few programmes which were recorded before the Orchestra left for the Continent. The date given is that of the broadcast; the recording date is unknown.

5 February 1945. A SOLDIER AND A SONG.

Where or When / In the Blue of Evening / Deep Purple / Sweet Lorraine.

STRINGS WITH WINGS.

You and the Night and the Music / Star Dust / Tico Tico / Over the Rainbow.

7 February 1945 STRINGS WITH WINGS.

April in Paris / Annie Laurie / Holiday with Strings.

9 FEBRUARY 1945. AMERICAN BAND OF THE A.E.F.

American Patrol / Body and Soul / I've got a Heart filled with Love for You, Dear / Medley: Mother Macree; I'm Making Believe; I can't give you anything but Love, Baby; Wang Wang Blues / Holiday for Strings.

THE UPTOWN HALL.

I'm coming Virginia / Louise/ What is this Thing called Love / I'll Walk Alone / You're Lucky to Me.

10 FEBRUARY 1945 THE UPTOWN HALL

China Boy / You got to my Head / I'm in the Mood for Love / The Earl.

12 FEBRUARY 1945 AMERICAN BAND OF THE A.E.F.

Caribbean Clipper / I'll Walk Alone / Little Brown Jug / Rhapsody in Blue / The Victory Polka.

SWING SHIFT.

Anchors Aweigh / Little Brown Jug / I'll Walk Alone / With Malice Aforethought / Is you is or is you ain't My Baby.

17 FEBRUARY 1945 SWING SHIFT

On Wisconsin / Tuxedo Junction / I Dream of You / Spanish Shawl / Broman Bounce / The Music Stopped / Whatcha Know Joe? / Stealing Apples.

25 FEBRUARY 1945 AMERICAN BAND OF THE A.E.F.

It must be Jelly / I only have Eyes for You Dear / Medley: Silver Threads among the Gold; Rainbow Corner; My Guy's Come Back; St. Louis Blues / Waiting for the Evening Mail / Meadowlands.

26 FEBRUARY 1945 SWING SHIFT

I Hear You Screaming / Sleepy Town Train / Blues in the Night—March / Trayful of Blues / Chatanooga Choo Choo / Time waits for No-one / Waiting for the Evening Mail / An Old Army March.

28 FEBRUARY 1945 A SOLDIER AND A SONG.

Time on my Hands / Spring will be a little late this year / The Lamp is Low / Deep Summer Music.

STRINGS WITH WINGS.

Someone to watch over me / Danny Boy / Bess, you is My Gal Now / Embraceable You.

4 MARCH 1945 AMERICAN BAND OF THE A.E.F.

Mission to Moscow / Deep Summer Music / Song of the Volga Boatmen / Medley: Mighty like a Rose / Amor, Amor; Chatanooga Choo Choo; Bye Bye Blues / Sweet Georgia Brown / Oranges and Lemons.

11 MARCH 1945 AMERICAN BAND OF THE A.E.F.

Caribbean Clipper / Together. VR, JD / String of Pearls / Medley: Killarney; Rainbow Corner VR, CC; Moonlight Serenade; Wabash Blues / Is you is or is you ain't My Baby? VR, RM / S'Wonderful (*Quartet;* Hucko, Powell, Alpert, McKinley) / The Victory Polka. VR, JD, CC, Ensemble.

Note:—This programme certainly—and perhaps some, or all, of the others listed here—were played on the Continent.—*G.E.B.*

UNKNOWN DATE UNIT UNKNOWN

As Happy as the Day is Long / Magic in the Moonlight / Swinging down the Road / Day in Day Out.

UNKNOWN DATE (played on Continent)
AMERICAN BAND OF THE A.E.F.

Here We Go Again / My Prayer. VR, JD / And her Tears flowed like Wine. VR, RM / Medley: Schubert's Serenade; Some Other Time; VR, JD; I've Got Sixpence. VR, AM, Ensemble; Rhapsody in Blue / String of Pearls / The Trolley Song. VR, JD, CC, Ensemble.

UNKNOWN DATE AMERICAN BAND OF THE A.E.F.

In the Mood/ More and More. VR, JD/Get Happy/ Medley: Old Black Joe; I've Got the Blues. VR, JD; Little Brown Jug; Under a Blanket of Blue/ No Compree/With My Head in the Clouds. VR, JD, E.

UNKNOWN DATE THE SWING SHIFT.

Somebody's wrong / Whatcha Know Joe? / I Dream of You. VR, JD / Plain and Fancy Blues / Choo Choo Baby. VR, CC / Time alone will Tell. VR, JD / My Guy's Come Back / Everybody Loves My Baby.

UNKNOWN DATE THE SWING SHIFT

I hear you Screaming / Sleepy Town Train / You, Fascinating You. VR, JD / S'Wonderful / Nine-Twenty Special / She's Funny That Way. VR, JD / Waiting for the Evening Mail. VR, RM / The Eyes and Ears of the World

---

THE UPTOWN HALL" (The Swing Sextet, led by Sgt. Mel Powell)

TB Glenn Miller (rarely);
TP Bernie Priven, Zeke Zarchey;
S Peanuts Hucko, Clt & TS, Hank Freeman, AS;
Rh Mel Powell, P; Trigger Alpert, B; Carmen Mastren, G; Ray McKinley, D.

Note:—The full Uptown Hall Group also used French horn, bass clarinet, and other unusual instruments.—*G.E.B.*

The following is a short list of air checks from English broadcasts.

After You've Gone
As long as I live
Blow Top
Blue Room
Body and Soul
Charmaine
Cheese Cake
China Boy
Don't Blame Me
The Earl
Flying Home
Fruit Cake
How high the Moon
I'il remember April
I must have that Man
I want to be happy
Jerry's Aachen back
Jubilee
Lady be Good
Liza
Love is the sweetest thing
My Guy's Come Back (*theme of the Uptown hall*)
No Compree.
One two button your shoe
Parachute Jump
Please don't talk about me when I'm gone
Rosetta
Shandy
Sheik of Araby.
Stars fell on Alabama
Sunny Side of the Street
Sweet Georgia Brown
Sweet Lorraine.
S'Wonderful
Train Eighty-eight
Triple-X.
Way down yonder in New Orleans
What is this thing called Love
With malice in my heart
You go to my Head.
You turned the tables on Me.

April 1945

While the A.E.F. Orchestra was in Paris, some of the men (the Swing Sextet) got together and cut some sides for the Jazz Club Francais. These discs were issued in France on the Jazz Club Francais label, and, later, in Belgium on the Victory Label, and in England on the Esquire label. The English Esquire issues were labelled as by "Glenn Miller's Uptown Hall Gang." (An interesting account of this session appeared in "The Record Exchange" (Toronto, October, 1951).—*G.E.B.*).

An official U.S. Signal Corps photo gives the following personnel:
TP Bernie Priven, Harry Cooper;
S Alex Campbell, TS; Hubert Rostains, Clt; Peanuts Hucko, Clt & TS;
Rh Mel Powell, P; Trigger Alpert, B; Carmen Mastren, Django Reinhardt, G; Jack O'Connor, Vibes; Ray McKinley, D.

Note:—So far as is known, the only one besides the Miller A.E.F. sidemen who actually played on the records was Django Reinhart, and he only played on some.—*G.E.B.*

1227 **How High the Moon.** **JCF 120,** Esq 10-043
1228 **If Dreams Come True.** **JCF 121,** Esq 10-087
1229 **Beating the Halleluja Drums.** **JCF 122,**
Victy 9032, Esq 10-243 (labelled as Halleluja).
1230 **Stomping at the Savoy.** **JCF 123,** Esq 10-043.
1231 **I Must Have that Man.** **JCF 122,**
Victy 9044, Esq 10-097.
1232 **Please don't talk about me when I'm gone.** **JCF 120,**
Victy 9032, Esq 10-053.
1233 **S'Wonderful.** **JCF 123,** Esq 10-097
1234 **Someday Sweetheart.** **JCF 120,** Esq-10-53
1235 **Blue Skies.** **JCF 121,**
Victy 9044, Esq 10-087.

1356 **Red Light.** **JCF 132,**
Victy 9045, Esq 10-243.
1357 **You're Driving Me Crazy.** **JCF 132,**
Victy 9059, Esq 10-209.
1358 **Indiana.** **JCF 133,** Victy 9045.
1359 **On the Sunny Side of the Street.** **JCF 133,** Esq 10-209.

P Mel Powell (*solos*)
1368 **Homage to Fats Waller.** **JCF 140,**
Victy 9046, Esq 10-199.
1369 **Homage to Debussy.** **JCF 140,**
Victy 9046, Esq 10-199.
1370 **For "Miss Black."** **JCF 141,**
Victy 9047, Esq 10-086.
1371 **Don't Blame Me.** **JCF 141,**
Victy 9047, Esq 10-086.

Full personnel again.

1372 **Pennies from Heaven.** **JCF 134,** Esq 10-149.
1373 **One, Two, Button your Shoe.** **JCF 135,** Esq 10-240.
1374 **At Sundown.** **JCF 134,** Esq 10-149.
1375 **Stealing Smack's Apples.** **JCF 135,** Esq 10-240.

Clt "Peanuts" Hucko;
P Mel Powell;
D Ray McKinley.

1376 **Sugar.** **JCF 130,** Victy 9057, Esq 10-070.
1377 **After You've Gone.** **JCF 130,** Victy 9057, Esq 10-070.
1378 **Shoemaker's Apron.** **JCF 131,** Victy 9058, Esq 10-150.
1379 **China Boy.** **JCF 131,** Victy 9058, Esq 10-150.

Note:—JCF issues labelled as Jazz Club Mystery Hot Band.
Esquire issues labelled as Glenn Miller's Uptown Hall Gang.
Trio titles labelled as Ray McKinley Trio.

The following programmes were conducted by Sgt. Jerry Gray after the Orchestra's tour of Europe.

5 June 1945 AMERICAN BAND OF THE A.E.F.

American Patrol / More and More / Mission to Moscow / Medley: Flow Gently, Sweet Afton; Moondreams; Don't be that way; Blue Champagne / Swing Low Sweet Chariot / Poinciana.

3 July 1945 AMERICAN BAND OF THE A.E.F.

Limehouse Blues / Embraceable You / American Patrol / Medley: Carry me back to Old Virginny; Some other Time; Alouette; Blue Moon / The Spirit is willing / Can't Help Singing.

8 July 1945. SWING SHIFT (cond. RMcK)

I can hear my Baby screaming / String of Pearls / You, Fascinating You / Jeep Jockey Jump / Accentuate the Positive / Get in There / My Buddy / Wooden Tub Jump.

17 July 1945 AMERICAN BAND OF THE A.E.F.

This was the final Miller programme on the A.E.F. Programme.

Juke Box Saturday Night / Stardust / Chatanooga Choo Choo / Rhapsody in Blue / Amor, Amor / My Buddy / The Anvil Chorus / Moonlight Serenade.

12 August 1945.

The Orchestra arrived back in New York.
For a while they resumed the "I Sustain the Wings" broadcasts. The Orchestra disintegrated gradually as the musicians were demobilised.

November 1945—Washington.

The Orchestra's last public performance was at the National Press Club dinner, attended by President Truman and General Eisenhower. Ray McKinley was recalled from civilian life to front the Orchestra.

Photo *His Master's Voice*

Major Glenn Miller and singer Dinah Shore in the H.M.V. recording studio in London, September 16, 1944, when Dinah made some recordings accompanied by Major Miller's American Band of the A.E.F. The A.E.F. Band also recorded two items from its own

Photo *U.S. Air Force*

Major Glenn Miller and his American Band of the A.E.F. entertaining U.S. servicemen at Steeple Morden, Cambridgeshire, England, on August 12, 1944. The trumpet soloist front and centre is M/Sgt. Reuben "Zeke" Zarchey.

SECTION V.

LONG PLAY ISSUES AND RE-ISSUES

(a) Commercial Releases.

In 1951 RCA Victor began issuing Glenn Miller selections on LP and EP. Some of these discs were merely reissues of existing masters, while others were air checks of the "Chesterfield" broadcasts. These air checks were released to R.C.A. Victor in September 1951 by the Glenn Miller Estate from Glenn's private reference library.

I am listing the LP's and EP's numerically in order to clear up any confusion. Where an album has been issued on LP and EP, the EP number is given in brackets. The selections reissued from Victor's vaults are indicated (+).

LPM-31 — GLENN MILLER AND HIS ORCHESTRA
- Pt. 1 — American Patrol (+) / In the Mood (+) / Stardust (+)
- Pt. 2 — Pennsylvania 6-5000 (+) / Little Brown Jug (+) / Song of The Volga Boatmen (+).

LPT-2 — DANCE BAND HITS
- Pt. 1 — Song of the Volga Boatmen (+) (This is the only Miller cut)

LPT-12 — UP SWING.
- Pt. 1 — Tuxedo Junction (+)
- Pt. 2 — String of Pearls (+)

} These are the only Miller cuts on this disc.

LPT-16 — GLENN MILLER CONCERT—Volume I. (EPBT-3025)
- Pt. 1 — One O'Clock Jump / Goin' Home / St. Louis Blues / Tiger Rag.
- Pt. 2 — Everybody loves my baby / Georgia on my mind / Jersey Bounce / My Blue Heaven / Moonlight Serenade.

LPT-30 — GLENN MILLER CONCERT—Volume II (EPBT-3026)
- Pt. 1 — Anchors Aweigh / My Buddy / I got Rhythm / I Dream of Jeannie with the Light Brown Hair.
- Pt. 2 — Vilia / Limehouse Blues / On the Alamo / On Brave Old Army Team.

LPT-3001 — GLENN MILLER CONCERT—Volume III (EPBT-3001)
- Pt. 1 — Dippermouth Blues / April in Paris / Are you Rusty, Gate? / Tchaikovsky's Piano Concerto.
- Pt. 2 — Fan Hat Stomp / Sleepy Lagoon/ Introduction to a waltz / Intermezzo.

LPT-3002 — THIS IS GLENN MILLER AND HIS ORCHESTRA—Volume 1 (EPBT-3002)
- Pt. 1 — Johnson Rag (+) / My Isle of Golden Dreams (+) / Anvil Chorus (+)
- Pt. 2 — Beautiful Ohio (Waltz) (+) / Pavanne (+) / Danny Boy (+)/ Adios (+)

LPT-3036 — THIS IS GLENN MILLER—Volume II (EPBT-3036).
- Pt. 1 — Sunrise Serenade (+) / Bugle Call Rag (+) / Tuxedo Junction (+) / String of Pearls (+).
- Pt. 2 — By the Waters of Minnetonka (+) / Runnin' Wild (+) / Moonlight Serenade (+).

LPT-3057 GLENN MILLER PLAYS SELECTIONS FROM "THE GLENN MILLER STORY." (EPBT-3057)

Pt. 1 Moonlight Serenade (+) / American Patrol / Pennsylvania 6-5000 (+) / In the Mood (+).

Pt. 2 Tuxedo Junction (+) / St. Louis Blues / String of Pearls / Little Brown Jug.

LPT-3064 MUSIC FROM THE ORIGINAL SOUNDTRACK OF THE 20TH CENTURY-FOX FILM PRODUCTION "SUN VALLEY SERENADE" PLAYED BY GLENN MILLER AND HIS ORCHESTRA (EPBT-3064).

Pt. 1 It happened in Sun Valley / In the Mood / At Last / Chatanooga Choo Choo.

Pt. 2 I Know Why / Sun Valley Jump / Measure for Measure / The Spirit is Willing.

LPT-3065 MUSIC FROM THE ORIGINAL SOUNDTRACK OF THE 20TH CENTURY-FOX FILM "ORCHESTRA WIVES" PLAYED BY GLENN MILLER AND HIS ORCHESTRA (EPBT-3065)

Pt. 1 American Patrol / Serenade in Blue / That's Sabotage / Moonlight Sonata.

Pt. 2 Kalamazoo / People like you and me / Bugle Call Rag.

LPT-3067 SUNRISE SERENADE. (EPBT-3067)

Pt. 1 Sunrise Serenade (+) / Bugle Call Rag (+) / Delilah (+) / By the waters of the Minnetonka (+).

Pt. 2 Running Wild /(+) Stardust (+) / Song of the Volga Boatmen (+) / Ida (+) / Don't sit under the Apple Tree (+).

LPT-1016 (12-in) JUKE BOX SATURDAY NIGHT.

Pt. 1 Chatanooga Choo Choo (+) / Kalamazoo (+) / Juke Box Saturday Night (+) / Elmer's Tune (+) / Perfidia (+) / Serenade in Blue (+).

Pt. 2 Moonlight Cocktail (+) / At Last (+) / Blue Evening (+) / Alice Blue Gown (+) / Missouri Waltz (+) / That Old Black Magic (+).

LPT-1031 (12-in) THE NEARNESS OF YOU

Pt. 1 The Nearness of You (+) / The Spirit is Willing (+) / April played the Fiddle (+) / To You (+) / Long Tall Mama (+) / Blue Rain (+).

Pt. 2 Moonlight Becomes You (+) / Rainbow Rhapsody (+) / Vagabond Dreams (+) / Story of a Starry Night (+) / Faithful to You (+) / Take the "A" Train (+).

Finally, Columbia issued some old Miller cuts from their "Brunswick" masters They issued them on their new "Epic" label.

Epic LG-1008 GLENN MILLER (Epic EG-1008)

Pt. 1 Community Swing / Humoresque / Dippermouth Blues / Doin' the Jive.

Pt. 2 I Got Rhythm / Time on My Hands / Sleepy Time Gal / Sold American.

Meanwhile, RCA Victor had issued single EP's.

EPA-148 GLENN MILLER

Pt. 1 American Patrol (+) / Song of the Volga Boatmen (+)

Pt. 2 In the Mood (+) / Little Brown Jug (+).

EPAT-401 JUKE BOX SATURDAY NIGHT.
Pt. 1 Chatanooga Choo Choo (+) / Kalamazoo (+)
Pt. 2 Juke Box Saturday Night (+) / That Old Black Magic (+).

EPAT-405 FOUR STAR.
Pt. 1 Stardust (+) / Pennsylvania 6-5000 (+)
Pt. 2 Missouri Waltz (+) / Alice Blue Gown (+)

EPAT-426 AH, SPRING.
Pt. 1 April Played the Fiddle (+) / Blue Rain (+)
Pt. 2 Vagabond Dreams (+) / Story of a Starry Night (+)

EPAT-427 THE NEARNESS OF YOU
Pt. 1 The Nearness of You (+) / To You (+)
Pt. 2 Moonlight becomes you (+) / Faithful to You (+).

EPAT-428 THE SPIRIT IS WILLING
Pt. 1 The Spirit is willing (+) / Long Tall Mama (+)
Pt. 2 Rainbow Rhapsody (+) / Take the "A" Train (+).

EPAT-429 ELMER'S TUNE
Pt. 1 At Last (+) / Blue Evening (+)
Pt. 2 Delilah (+) / Elmer's Tune. (+)

EPAT-430 MOONLIGHT COCKTAILS
Pt. 1 Moonlight Cocktails (+) / Perfidia (+)
Pt. 2 Serenade in Blue (+) / It happened in Hawaii (+)

Late in 1954, Victor issued a series of Extended Play 45's entitled "Honor Roll of Hits," some of which contained Miller cuts as follows:

EPA-527 HONOR ROLL OF HITS 1939
Sunrise Serenade (+) / Wishing (+)
Deep Purple (WILL GLAHE) / Beer Barrel Polka (HUGO WINTERHALTER).

EPA-528 HONOR ROLL OF HITS 1940
Woodpecker Song (+) / In the Mood (+)
Tuxedo Junction (+) / I'll never smile again (TOMMY DORSEY).

EPA-529 HONOR ROLL OF HITS 1941
Chatanooga Choo Choo (+) / Amapola (SAMMY KAYE).
Tschaikovsky's Piano Concerto (FREDDY MARTIN) / Frenesi (ARTIE SHAW)

EPA-530 HONOR ROLL OF HITS 1942
Kalamazoo (+) / Who wouldn't love you (TOMMY DORSEY).
Moonlight Cocktails (+) / Sleepy Lagoon (FREDDY MARTIN)

THE GLENN MILLER LIMITED EDITION.

In October 1953 RCA Victor issued a tribute to Glenn Miller in the form of a limited edition album containing five 12-inch Long Play records. Some of the selections were issued previously on Bluebird and Victor, but many were unissued air checks from the "Chesterfield" broadcasts. Those from Victor vaults are indicated (+).

The album was a plush one with white leather covering and very excellent paper and printing inside.

A white-label EP was issued as a sales booster and is not for sale. Mr. George Frazier who put the album together is announcer on this disc. Parts of selections featured in the "Limited Edition" are on this disc. It is titled "HIGHLIGHTS FROM THE GREAT GLENN MILLER LIMITED EDITION—1953." There is no issue number.

E3VW 3349 (6: 52) Moonlight Serenade (+) / American Patrol / Babv Me (+) / String of Pearls / Boulder Buff (+) / On a little Street in Singapore (+) / Little Brown Jug.

E3VW 3350 (6: 22) Oh So Good / Say Si Si (+) / Sun Valley Jump (+) / Don't sit under the apple tree / Ida (+) / Farewell Blues / Moonlight Serenade (+).

THE LIMITED EDITION. LPT-6700 10-12-in. LP sides.

Side	*Master*	*Titles*	*Label No.*
1.	E3VP 5236	Moonlight Serenade (+) / Perfidia / Wonderful one / Weekend of a Private Secretary / Always in my heart (+) / Boulder Buff (+).	LPT-6700-1
2.	E3VP 5237	Caribbean Clipper (+) / Make Believe / Say Si Si (+) / Introduction to a Waltz / Medley: Japanese Sandman; What's the matter with me; Let's Dance; Blue Room / Down for the Count.	LPT-6700-2
3.	E3VP 5238	Rainbow Rhapsody (+) / Little Brown Jug / Imagination (+) / It Must be Jelly / Devil May Care (+) / Chip off the old block (+)	LPT-6700-3
4.	E3VP 5239	American Patrol / Ida (+) / I guess I'll have to Change my Plans / Glen Island Special (+)/ Medley: My Darling; Blueberry Hill; I can't get started / Bugle Call Rag.	LPT-6700-4
5.	E3VP 5240	Little Street in Singapore (+) / Oh So Good / Baby Me (+) / There'll be some changes made / Medley: Moon over Miami; Million Dreams Ago; Aloha / Sun Valley Jump (+).	LPT-6700-5
6.	E3VP 5241	String of Pearls / Love with a Capital You (+) Wishing will make it so (+) / Rug Cutter's Swing (+) / Angel Child (+) / King Porter Stomp.	LPT-6700-5
7.	E3VP 5242	Chatanooga Choo Choo / Medley: My Melancholy Baby; Moon Love; Stompin' at the Savoy; Blue Moon / Sleepy Town Train (+) My Devotion / Fresh as a daisy / Flag waver	LPT-6700-4
8.	E3VP 5243	One O'Clock Jump / Don't sit under the Apple Tree / Lady be Good / Fools rush in (+) / Twenty-four Robbers / The Hop.	LPT-6700-3
9.	E3VP 5244	Careless (+) / Naughty Sweetie Blues / Bless You / Sweet Eloise (+) / Rhapsody in Blue (+) / Slip Horn Jive (+).	LPT-6700-2
10.	E3VP 5245	Here we go again (+) / Mister Meadowlark (+) / Little bit south of North Carolina / Under a Blanket of Blue / Lamplighter's Serenade (+) / Farewell Blues / Moonlight Serenade (+).	LPT-6700-1

Note:—The Limited Edition was issued in Europe on five 12-in. LPs in a special Album, by His Master's Voice in December 1954, as Record Library Series No. 599—*G.E.B.*

THE LIMITED EDITION EBNT-6700 28-7-in. EP. sides.

Side	*Master*	*Titles*	*Label No.*
1.	E3PW 1546	Moonlight Serenade (+) / Perfidia / Wonderful One—Waltz (+).	947-0116-A
2.	E3PW 1547	Weekend of a Private Secretary / Always in my Heart (+).	947-0117-A
3.	E3PW 1548	Boulder Buff (+) / Caribbean Clipper (+)	947-0118-A
4.	E3PW 1549	Make Believe / Say Si Si (+) / Introduction a Waltz.	947-0119-A
5.	E3PW 1550	Medley: Japanese Sandman; What's the matter with me; Let's Dance; Blue Room / Down for the Count.	947-0120-A
6.	E3PW 1551	Rainbow Rhapsody (+) / Little Brown Jug	947-0121-A
7.	E3PW 1552	Imagination (+) / It must be Jelly	947-0122-A
8.	E3PW 1553	Devil May Care (+) / Chip off the old block (+)	947-0123-A
9.	E3PW 1554	American Patrol / Ida (+)	947-0124-A
10.	E3PW 1555	Guess I'll have to change my plans / Glen Island Special (+)	947-0125-A
11.	E3PW 1556	Medley: My Darling; Blueberry Hill; I can't Get Started / Bugle Call Rag	947-0126-A
12.	E3PW 1557	Little Street in Singapore (+) / Oh So Good	947-0127-A
13.	E3PW 1558	Baby Me (+) / There'll be some changes made	947-0128-A
14.	E3PW 1559	Medley: Moon over Miami; A million dreams Ago; Aloha / Sun Valley Jump (+).	947-0129-A
15.	E3PW 1573	String of Pearls / Love with a Capital You (+)	947-0129-B
16.	E3PW 1572	Wishing Will Make it So (+) / Rug Cutter's Swing (+).	947-0128-B
17.	E3PW 1571	Angel Child (+) / King Porter Stomp	947-0127-B
18.	E3PW 1570	Chatanooga Choo Choo / Medley: My Melancholy Baby; Moon Love; Stompin' at the Savoy; Blue Moon.	947-0126-B
19.	E3PW 1569	Sleepy Town Train (+) / My Devotion / Fresh as a daisy.	947-0125-B
20.	E3PW 1568	Flag Waver / One O'Clock Jump	947-0124-B
21.	E3PW 1567	Don't sit under the apple tree / Lady be good	947-0123-B
22.	E3PW 1566	Fools Rush In (+) / Twenty-four Robbers	947-0122-B
23.	E3PW 1565	The Hop / Careless (+)	947-0121-B
24.	E3PW 1564	Naughty Sweetie Blues / Bless You	947-0120-B
25.	E3PW 1563	Sweet Eloise (+) / Rhapsody in Blue (+)	947-0119-B
26.	E3PW 1562	Slip Horn Jive (+) / Here we go again (+)	947-0118-B
27.	E3PW 1561	Mister Meadowlark (+) / Just a little bit south of North Carolina / Under a blanket of Blue.	947-0117-B
28.	E3PW 1560	Lamplighter's Serenade (+) / Farewell Blues / Moonlight Serenade (+).	947-0116-B

THE GLENN MILLER LIMITED EDITION VOLUME 2.

In October 1954, RCA Victor issued a second Album containing five 12-inch LP's consisting entirely of air checks of the Band's various broadcasts from June 1938 to September 1942. The Album was a plush, padded one, similar to the first, and contained photographs, a Discography (which contained a number of errors of personnel), and descriptive notes by George Frazier.

A black label EP was issued as a sales booster and is not for sale. It contains parts of selections featured in the "Limited Edition Vol 2," announced by Mr. Frazier. It is entitled "Highlights from the Great Glenn Miller Limited Edition, Vol. 2, 1954," and the number is SPA-7-4.

Note:—The Limited Edition Vol 2 was scheduled for issue in Europe on 5 12-inch LPs in a special Album by His Master's Voice in 1956 as Record Library Series No. 598 *G.E.B.*

Side 1 E4VH-0581 (5: 05) *Excerpts from* Hallelujah / I'm sorry for myself / In a Sentimental Mood.

Side 2 E4VH-0582 (5: 39) *Excerpts from* Tiger Rag / Deep in the heart of Texas / Pagan Love Song.

THE LIMITED EDITION VOL. 2 LPT-6701 10-12-in LP sides.

Side	*Master*	*Titles*	*Label No.*
1.	E4VP-8201	Along the Santa Fe Trail / Swinging at the Seance / In a sentimental mood / Frenesi / Isn't that just like love / I dreamt I dwelt in Harlem.	LPT-6701-1
2.	E4VP-8202	You walked by / Are you Jumping Jack? / A million dreams ago / Daisy Mae / Falling Leaves / Crosstown.	LPT-6701-2
3.	E4VP-8203	At Sundown / My last Goodbye / Hallelujah / The Hour of Parting / I'm Sorry for myself / The Jumping Jive.	LPT-6701-3
4.	E4VP-8204	Twilight Interlude / And the Angels sing / Sunrise Serenade / Blue Orchids / We can live on love / Pagan Love Song.	LPT-6701-4
5.	E4VP-8205	We've come a long way together / Get out of Town / Blue Skies / Heaven can wait / Bluebirds in the Moonlight / I want to be happy.	LPT-6701-5
6.	E4VP-8206	My heart belongs to Daddy / Deep Purple / After All / St. Louis Blues / Indian Summer / Tiger Rag.	LPT-6701-5
7.	E4VP-8207	Georgia on my Mind / Be Happy / I don't want to Walk without You / Limehouse Blues / Daddy / Deep in the heart of Texas.	LPT-6701-4
8.	EV4P-8208	Doing the Jive / This can't be Love / A stone's throw from Heaven / Humoresque / So Little Time / Down South Camp Meeting.	LPT-6701-3
9.	E4VP-8209	Anchors Aweigh / Body and Soul / Let's have another Cup of Coffee / The Rhumba Jumps / How deep is the Ocean / Measure for Measure.	LPT-6701-2
10.	E4VP-8210	On the Alamo / April in Paris / Dancing in A Dream / Sophisticated Lady /I'll never Smile Again / V for Victory Hop.	LPT-6701-1

THE LIMITED EDITION VOL. 2. EPOT-6701. 30—7-in. EP sides.

Side	Master	Titles	Label No.
1.	E4VH-0451	Along the Sante Fe Trail / Swinging at the Seance	947-0178-A
2.	E4VH-0452	In a Sentimental Mood / Frenesi	947-0179-A
3.	E4VH-0453	Isn't that just like love / I dreamt I dwelt in Harlem.	947-0180-A
4.	E4VH-0454	You walked by / Are you jumping Jack?	947-0181-A
5.	E4VH-0455	A Million Dreams Ago / Daisy Mae	947-0182-A
6.	E4VH-0456	Falling Leaves / Crosstown	947-0183-A
7.	E4VH-0457	At Sundown / My Last Goodbye	947-0184-A
8.	EV4H-0458	Hallelujah / The hour of parting	947-0185-A
9.	E4VH-0459	I'm sorry for myself / The Jumping Jive.	947-0186-A
10.	E4VH-0460	Twilight Interlude / And the Angels Sing	947-0187-A
11.	E4VH-0461	Sunrise Serenade / Blue Orchids	947-0188-A
12.	E4VH-0462	We can live on love / Pagan Love Song	947-0189-A
13.	E4VH-0463	We've come a long way together / Get out of Town	947-0190-A
14.	E4VH-0464	Blue Skies / Heaven Can Wait.	947-0191-A
15.	E4VH-0465	Bluebirds in the moonlight / I want to be Happy	947-0192-A
16.	E4VH-0466	My heart belongs to Daddy / Deep Purple	947-0192-B
17.	E4VH-0467	After All / St. Louis Blues	947-0191-B
18.	E4VH-0468	Indian Summer / Tiger Rag	947-0190-B
19.	E4VH-0469	Georgia on my mind / Be Happy	947-0189-B
20.	E4VH-0470	I don't want to walk without you / Limehouse Blues	947-0188-B
21.	E4VH-0471	Daddy / Deep in the heart of Texas	947-0187-B
22.	E4VH-0472	Doing the Jive / This can't be love	947-0186-B
23.	E4VH-0473	A Stone's Throw from Heaven / Humoresque	947-0185-B
24.	E4VH-0474	So little Time / Down South Camp Meeting	947-0184-B
25.	E4VH-0475	Anchors Aweigh / Body and Soul	947-0183-B
26.	E4VH-0476	Let's have another Cup of Coffee / The Rhumba Jumps.	947-0182-B
27.	E4VH-0477	How deep is the Ocean / Measure for Measure	947-0181-B
28.	E4VH-0478	On the Alamo / April in Paris	947-0180-B
29.	E4VH-0479	Dancing in a Dream / Sophisticated Lady	947-0179-B
30.	E4VH-0480	I'll never smile again / V for Victory Hop	947-0178-B

THE GLENN MILLER ARMY AIR FORCE BAND ALBUM

This Album is Listed in full in label order on pages 70-72.

(b) "Glenn Miller's Moonlight Serenade" Transcriptions

These are 16-in. 33-1/3 rpm radio program transcriptions (available to radio stations) which have been dubbed from air checks of Glenn's original "Chesterfield" programs broadcast from 27 December 1939 until 29 September, 1942. The majority of the selections are introduced by Glenn himself, or by the network announcer Larry Bruff. Where the broadcast dates are known they are listed in Section III of this booklet.

Each program is introduced and closed by Del Sharbutt, backed by Glenn's familiar theme, "Moonlight Serenade." Most of the transcriptions were compiled and made available during 1951 by Miller Transcriptions Inc., Hollywood, California.

GMMS 1	Sophisticated Lady / Boog Street / April played the Fiddle / Tiger Rag /
GMMS 2	Guess I'll have to change my plans / My Darling / Blueberry Hill/ I can't get started / Blue / My Blue Heaven.
GMMS 3	Pennsylvania 6-5000 / Let's all sing together / Moonlight Serenade/ Slip Horn Jive.
GMMS 4	Johnson Rag / I'll never Smile Again / Wham / Fan Hat Stomp
GMMS 5 } GMMS 53	Outside of that I love you / The gentleman needs a shave / When the Swallows come back to Capistrano / Everybody loves My Baby.
GMMS 6 } GMMS 54	T'aint no use at all / Goodnight Sweetheart/ I'm Stepping out with a Memory Tonight / When my Baby smiles at Me / A Blues Serenade / Runnin' Wild.
GMMS 7 } 55	Rug Cutter's Swing / Polka Dots and Moonbeams / FDR Jones / Drink to me only with thine eyes / Runnin' Wild
GMMS 8 } GMMS 56	Wham / Peg O' My Heart / Polka Dots and Moonbeams / Mood Indigo / Blue Orchids / Down for the Count.
GMMS 9 } GMMS 57	On the Aiamo / Cabana in Havana / I'll never smile again / St. Louis Blues.
GMMS 10 } GMMS 58	My Isle of Golden Dreams / Devil May Care / Let's all Sing Together / Everybody Loves my Baby.
GMMS 11 } GMMS 59	Oh Lady be Good / I'll Never Smile Again / Say Si Si / My Blue Heaven
GMMS 12 } GMMS 60	One O'Clock Jump / When you wish upon a star / Be Happy / On Brave Old Army Team.
GMMS 13 } GMMS 61	Jeannie with the Light Brown Hair / Outside of that I Love You / Handful of Stars / King Porter Stomp
GMMS 14 } GMMS 62	Sunrise Serenade / The Gentleman needs a Shave / The Story of a Starry Night / In the Mood
GMMS 15 } GMMS 63	Star Dust / Can't you hear me calling, Caroline? / Sweet Potato Piper / Pagan Love Song
GMMS 16 } GMMS 64	Say Si Si / Goodnight Sweetheart / I'm Stepping out with a Memory, tonight / When my Baby Smiles at Me / A Blues Serenade / Bugle Call Rag
GMMS 17 } GMMS 65	Rug Cutter's Swing / Outside of that I Love You / String of Pearls / Slip Horn Jive.
GMMS 18 } GMMS 66	Conversation Piece/ I wanna Hat with Cherries / Polka Dots and Moonbeams / St. Louis Blues.
GMMS 19 } GMMS 67	On the Alamo / Let's all Sing Together / Say It / Fan Hat Stomp
GMMS 20 } GMMS 68	Jeannie with the Light Brown Hair / I Never Took a Lesson in My Life / When the Swallows come back to Capistrano / I want to be Happy.

GMMS 21 GMMS 69	Largo / Bugle Boogie / You Walk By / Oh So Good
GMMS 22 GMMS 70	The Woodpecker Song / Poor Butterfly / The Sky Fell Down / I'm Getting Sentimental over You / Black and Blue / By the Waters of the Minnetonka.
GMMS 23 GMMS 71	Anchors Aweigh / Fools Rush In / The Weekend of a Private Secretary / Tuxedo Junction.
GMMS 24 GMMS 72	My Buddy / Wham / High on a windy hill / Caribbean Clipper.
GMMS 25 GMMS 73	Whatcha Know Joe? / Dancing in a Dream / Boog It / Are you Rusty, Gate?
GMMS 26 GMMS 74	On the Alamo / A love song hasn't been Sung / A little bit South of North Carolina / Here we go again.
GMMS 27 GMMS 75	Slow Freight / Fools Rush In / Woodpecker Song / King Porter Stomp.
GMMS 28 GMMS 76	I want to be Happy / Cowboy from Brooklyn / Sierra Sue / In the Mood.
GMMS 29 GMMS 77	I'll take you Home again, Kathleen / I haven't time to be a Millionaire / I'll Never Smile Again / Down for the Count.
GMMS 30 GMMS 78	Solitude / Be Happy / I'm Stepping out with a Memory Tonight/ My Blue Heaven.
GMMS 31 GMMS 79	My My / My Darling / Blueberry Hill / I can't get started with You / Blue / Tuxedo Junction.
GMMS 32 GMMS 80	What's your Story, Morning Glory? / I wanna Hat with Cherries/ Fools Rush In / Solid as a Stone Wall, Jackson.
GMMS 33 GMMS 81	Little Brown Jug / I wouldn't take a Million / A Tisket, A Tasket/ Farewell Blues.
GMMS 34 GMMS 82	Window Shopping on Fifth Avenue / In the Mood / The Nearness of You / Runnin' Wild.
GMMS 35 GMMS 83	Caprice / Outside of that I love you / Blueberry Hill / Everybody Loves My Baby.
GMMS 36 GMMS 84	In the Gloaming / Five O'Clock Whistle / Trade Winds / Down for the Count.
GMMS 37	Sophisticated Lady / A Cowboy from Brooklyn / Call of the Canyon / Pennsylvania 6-5000.
GMMS 38	The Gentleman needs a Shave / Isn't it Romantic / Shadows on the Sand / Blue Prelude / Tiger Rag.
GMMS 39	My Buddy / Polka Dots and Moonbeams / FDR Jones / Volga Boatmen.
GMMS 40	One O'clock Jump / When you wish upon a Star/ Cabana in Havana / Caribbean Clipper.
GMMS 41	I Guess I'll have to Change my Plans / My Darling / Blueberry Hill / I can't started / Blue / Sliphorn Jive.

GMMS 42 Sunrise Serenade / Let's all Sing Together / April played the Fiddle / Fan Hat Stomp.

GMMS 43 Rug Cutter's Swing / Boog It / When the Swallows come back to Capistrano / My Blue Heaven.

GMMS 44 T'ain't No Use At All / Goodnight Sweetheart / I'm Stepping out with a Memory Tonight / When My Baby Smiles at Me / A Blues Serenade / Bugle Call Rag.

GMMS 45 Stardust / I wanna Hat with Cherries / Story of a Starry Night / Tuxedo Junction.

GMMS 46 Conversation Piece / When you Wish upon a Star / Be Happy / String of Pearls.

GMMS 47 Jeannie with the Light Brown Hair / Peg O' My Heart / Polka Dots and Moonbeams / Mood Indigo / Blue Orchids / St. Louis Blues.

GMMS 48 On the Alamo / Can't you hear me Calling, Caroline / Handful of Stars / On Brave Old Army Team.

GMMS 49 Solitude / My My / You Walked By / Song of the Volga Boatmen.

GMMS 50 Whatcha Know Joe? / Fools Rush In / Weekend of a Private Secretary / Oh So Good.

GMMS 51 Largo / Poor Butterfly / The Sky Fell Down / I'm Getting Sentimental over You / Black and Blue / Slip Horn Jive.

GMMS 52 Slow Freight / Just a little bit South of North Carolina / High on Windy Hill / Pagan Love Song.

INDEX TO TUNE TITLES

Note—This Index includes only those recordings which have actually existed as gramophone records available to individuals, i.e. commercial issues (including broadcasts) and the V-Discs and A.F.N. L.P.s.

Names of the artists under whose names the records were issued are given in brackets, and the following abbreviations are used:

AAF	Miller Army Air Force Band.
AFN	Miller A.F.N. "Bootleg" L.P.s.
CC	Charleston Chasers.
LRK	Louisiana Rhythm Kings.
MCBB	Mound City Blueblowers.
S/T	film soundtrack recording.
UH	Miller Uptown Hall small group.
V-D	Miller A.A.F. V-Discs.

Titles with no artist name are Miller civilian records.

Titles beginning with "the" or "a" are indexed under the next word in the title.

Titles printed in italics are broadcast recordings.

References are to page numbers.